Contents

With gratitude to:

Irv Schwartz, my childhood friend, whose encouragement from afar, after changing careers himself, was catalytic to this endeavor.

Mike Collins, a youthful Princetonian in China who took me under his wing.

Chip Rountree, photographer of a recalcitrant thirteen-year-old, who is responsible for this book being judged by its cover.

Angie Baecker, who understands that it is not the devil which is in the detail, but the very substance itself.

Introduction

My abiding interest in *The Yijing* (The Book of Changes) has taught me that while a moment in time is indeed unique, it is nonetheless connected to all others, forming a net of phenomena that somehow binds all together. While the velocity of change in China is without precedent, I would be mistaken to style myself as Rip Van Winkle as I look back over these *Pieces of China*. Only if one dwells on the skyscrapers, posh cars, and reverence for MBAs amongst current students can the conclusion be reached that the present is truly disconnected from the past. Of greater significance than the bricks and mortar, which might seem to be dwarfing us all in China, is the absence of that lingering fear that had so permeated life during my sojourn here following the end of the Cultural Revolution. While other Beijing returnees voice valid regret over the loss of great swathes of hutong, I prefer to marvel at the simple pleasure of being able to visit a friend's home. Society can hardly be described as open—the police did pay us a visit to check out our immigration status prior to the Olympics—but the warmth and playfulness of local folks, so brutally stifled by the politics of madness, are once again happily abroad. Such qualities have not been created, but merely recovered.

These stories about my student days in Taiwan, first visit to China, pioneering days at work in Beijing, and an adventure in Tibet are all of a cloth in my mind. I began writing them during a summer on Shelter Island, and my Smythson notebook gradually filled up over time. Words tumbled forth either at a little table near the drug store or in subsequent business meetings in London and Beijing. Many who watched me in those conference rooms were terribly impressed by what they thought to be meticulous note taking. May *Pieces of China* turn out to be more evocative than those notes that were never written.

It is my hope that my daughters, born in China but citizens of the world, will have the pleasure of thinking that they, too, are all the more special for having had their Chinese experiences, and that the very uniqueness of it all will happily connect them to me in that hospitable net of which they are already an unknowing part.

Beijing

Spring 2009

Black Shoes

In the early seventies, the closest an American could get to China was Taiwan; thus, to learn the language, it was quite natural to go off to study in the Republic of China (not to be confused with the People's Republic of China). Princeton had an academic relationship with Tunghai University in Taichung, so I went there to teach English and learn Chinese, as was the custom. Several American universities had similar arrangements; thus, there were others like me mixed amongst the Chinese teaching assistants, living in the *nan baigong* (the male white house). Right across the hall from me was Tom, a student from Oberlin College, who quickly became a pal. There were others from Oberlin on the same program; aside from Tom, I grew particularly fond of Annie and Harry, married students who lived in a little house amongst proper faculty down the road from our dormitory.

As the term wore on, people began discussing holiday plans. It only seemed natural that Tom and I decided to club together for an excursion. A friend of Tom's in Bangkok had invited him to visit, and I was welcomed to tag along; and Annie, a Hong Kong Chinese, suggested that we drop in on her parents during our maneuvers in Southeast Asia.

With the coming of winter, I understood well why everyone cleared out of the university. Perched on the side of Tatu Mountain beyond the city, the campus caught fierce winds and faced plummeting temperatures. The buildings, though beautifully built in the Tang style, were just not winterized. That the campus could boast I.M. Pei's first building of distinction, a chapel fashioned after hands clasped in prayer, did little to keep the faithful warm in the winter.

Tom and I came up with a plan to spend both Western and Chinese New Years in Hong Kong with Bangkok sandwiched in between. Annie was so welcoming and breezy about the prospect of our double visits that the notion of imposition, which had kept us tentative about committing, finally evaporated.

"Just give me your arrival details," was all she ever repeated when we inquired about transport, hotels, sightseeing, etc.

Since we would be spending New Year's Eve in Hong Kong, as well as some time visiting Tom's friend in Bangkok—whose father was a senior official with the United Nations in Thailand—the situation probably called for proper clothing. I had one of those machine-washable white Haspel suits that took up little room in a duffle bag well-stuffed with shorts and t-shirts. The prospect of leaving behind the padded brown silk scholar's gown (*changpao*), an affectation that nonetheless kept me very warm on the mountainside in windy Taichung, was a delight.

We first took the train to Taipei, the lively capital that always reminded seasoned Asia hands of Tokyo a quarter of a century earlier. Tom and I split up, planning to meet the following day. I headed for the Yung-ho section of the city where Dr. Ch'en and his family lived. I had been "adopted" by them upon arriving the summer before, introduced by a schoolmate from Princeton. A sprawling clan whose elders were just as comfortable speaking the local Chinese dialect as they were Japanese (they had grown up during the pre-war occupation), the Ch'ens had little to do with the sense of Chineseness I had internalized at Princeton. They hardly seemed the carriers of the Great Tradition, rescued from the mainland, along with porcelain, calligraphy, and bronzes. After all, the Ch'ens had been here before Chiang Kai-shek.

The family lived in a large cement building right across the Shuang Hsi River, reminding me of a structure built by distant relatives in Jerusalem. That house, in an empty place on King David Street, had stood out when it was constructed in Israel in the early twentieth century, only to be surrounded and overwhelmed by urban sprawl later. What started out as a homestead became a tenement amongst many. The same could be said of the Ch'en home in Taipei: rather than antique armoires made of exotic woods and calligraphy lining the walls of lantern-filled chambers, the house was dominated by a cavernous garage of a sitting room, occupied only by a fridge, motorbike, and ping-pong table. At first glance, I simply assumed that the family was struggling. That beds were lined up dormitory-style simply reinforced that notion. Yet somehow, cars would appear when needed, superb meals were always on offer, tickets to events were magically available, and clothes that fit would show up on my bed. There was, indeed, a Great Tradition to be discovered beyond the disoriented homemaking.

During my time spent with the Ch'ens, I was always being introduced to new crowds of relatives with whom I could barely communicate. Not only was my Mandarin elementary at best, but I knew not a word of Taiwanese, the local dialect related to the Fujian variety of Chinese spoken across the strait. What I did manage to pick up, though, was the custom of nicknames. After yet another one of these Ch'en family dinners, I screwed up my courage and asked for a Taiwanese nickname. When told that I would be given an appropriate one in due course, I got all misty about being accepted into the clan.

As it happened, the clan's very next plenary event coincided with my stop en route to Hong Kong. I was taken aside by one of the Ch'en brothers and told that a name had, indeed, been chosen. Then, playing upon my earlier display of emotion, he asked me if I would introduce myself to the whole crowd using my new name, as though the event were being transformed from a noisy meal into a rite of passage in my honor.

The name chosen was De Gong in Mandarin, meaning "Duke of Virtue," but pronounced Di Gong in Taiwanese. The room was called to silence and I was asked to stand. In halting Mandarin, I thanked the Ch'en family for their hospitality and proceeded to say that I finally had a Taiwanese nickname to share with everyone.

"Di Gong," I proclaimed, and the entire crowd immediately fell about laughing. Assuming the pronunciation to be flawed, I said it again, taking great pains to articulate the words in some alternative fashion that would surely get the people to understand me. The laughter continued. There I stood, bewildered. Suddenly, Dr. Ch'en's arm was around me, and he spoke to his guests. A round of applause ensued and I was immediately surrounded by people offering congratulations. I beamed, but had not a clue about what had transpired. It turned out that Di Gong in Taiwanese means "horny pig," and there I was, proudly identifying myself as one to the delight of all. For once, if only my pronunciation had not been so good, I might have escaped the humiliation of it all; but it didn't matter. I had been accepted and was thereafter known affectionately as Di Gong.

Tom and I were thrilled by the legendary approach to Kai Tak Airport in Hong Kong. After an abrupt bank to the right, we found ourselves amongst tenements, eye level with televisions and dinner tables, actually able to see plates being served as we passed over Kowloon City!

We then were able to make a swift exit from the airport since we had not checked any luggage. Emerging into the arrivals hall, a scene of Cantonese bedlam, we were somehow immediately identified by a driver who whisked us away to a waiting Mercedes-Benz—not exactly what I had expected while airborne.

The ride from the Kowloon side to Victoria Island, offering up skyscrapers, harbor views, and the simple intensity of Chinese life at eye level, was a riveting visual assault even to a jaded New Yorker. Once on the Hong Kong side, we made our way up a steep and curving roadway to Repulse Bay, finally turning into the gated drive of a very grand white house with terraced gardens. I later discovered this had been the residence of the last king of Vietnam, Bao Dai.

Our concerns about sleeping bags and sofas were nonsense, and Annie's warm and blasé attitude about hospitality suddenly made sense upon entering her home, which was hopping with activity. After briefly meeting her mother—more about her later—Tom and I were immediately separated and shown to our rooms. From afar, I kept hearing Mrs. Siu (called Ceil by Tom and me) barking something that sounded like "a-ha," which then apparently caused a wisp of an old woman in black pajamas and cloth shoes to appear in my room, where she then beckoned me to follow her down the stairs. I was led into the dining room for a late lunch, where Tom and I were reunited with Annie, Harry, and a bunch of other folks. More General Patton than Perle Mesta, Mrs. Siu, drifting from Cantonese to English to Mandarin, informed us of a big banquet at home that night and the plans for New Year's Eve—we would be attending the ball at the Repulse Bay Hotel.

Once dismissed, I ran right upstairs to rescue my white suit from the duffle bag. Clearly, it would be called for that night and needed to be refreshed. Since I knew neither how to iron nor felt comfortable asking anyone to help me out, I decided to turn on the shower full blast, leave the suit sealed in the bathroom, and hope for the best. I bided my time by reading a guidebook on Thailand until I reckoned the steam had done the trick. I then opened the bathroom door only to find that the trousers had slipped off the hanger onto the wet floor; they were no longer simply wrinkled, but now soaked as well. In a panic, I took the mattress off the bedsprings, sandwiched the trousers between towels, and threw this bundle on the bed before replacing the mattress, thereby hoping both to dry and press the trousers.

By the time I made it to supper, my world had narrowed to a trouser drama; nonetheless, there I was sitting at a table, one of about fifteen in the ballroom, all of which were groaning with food, flowers, silver, and crystal. The guests were a diverse lot, moving freely between languages and topics, and they graciously included me in small talk. I was seated between two formidable Chinese ladies, one significantly older than the other, with a gentleman known to them both, seated next to the elder of the two. The three of them chatted happily around me, and I finally found myself loosening up to the point of inquiring as to how they all knew each other.

"I'm Mrs. Wu and this is my son," I heard on my left.

"...and I was his father's last wife," came from my right.

I wasn't in Kansas anymore.

The following day, New Year's Eve, was spent sightseeing. As we wandered through alleys off of Cat Street well into the afternoon, it dawned on me that my white suit would somehow need to be transformed into an outfit that could get me through the door of the Repulse Bay Hotel. Though I knew little of Hong Kong, I had somehow heard of Lane Crawford, a posh emporium in Queen's Road Central. Since it was too late for me to buy a new suit, I decided that a new bow tie would be just the thing. Taking a detour to the shop, we still smelled of the burning coiled incense hanging from the ceiling at Man Mo Temple, our last port of call.

It was a good thing that all I wanted was a bow tie. Aside from the prices, to which I was determined not to react, nothing except a bow tie would have fit me in the entire store. In this outpost of Canton, populated by short people as opposed to the taller folks of northern China, the purchase of clothing was difficult indeed. I found my bow tie, though—an enormous navy, velvet butterfly of a bow tie—and left the place convinced that I would somehow prevail that evening. I had been taught, after all, that simply by being tall, the world could be my oyster.

The house was bustling when we got back and I grandly climbed the stairs, clutching the pretentious Lane Crawford bag.

I nonchalantly brushed past a black suit bag hanging on my room door as I went to unpack my bow tie. The white suit would do just fine, I reflected, enlivened by this velvet accessory. Now confident, I got curious and opened the garment bag only to find a tuxedo. Though unsure of its provenance, I decided to try it on. It fit perfectly. Then, I noticed a formal shirt, cuff links and studs, on the bed as well. At that moment, A-ha silently entered the room and made straight for the closet. She took out my only pair of shoes, the brown ones, sat down on the floor, produced a tiny alcohol lamp, lit it, and began rubbing in warm black polish, addressing my outfit's last imperfection. My brown shoes were no more.

There I was, the tallest in our group, in a tuxedo that fit like a glove, my bow tie serving me well and my brown shoes a secret. Our Anglo-Chinese party was certainly familiar with this annual occasion, with Hong Kong very much the rump of a barely extant British empire. I danced the night away with a girl named Gerry Mao who had come home from England just in time for the event. I felt somehow obliged to be cool about the ball in an effort to match the elegant ease of my dancing partner—old beer for her, but a cosmic thrill for this New York hick.

Within a few days, Tom and I were back in the Mercedes, on our way to the airport for a stay in Bangkok with Jesse, Tom's friend from college. We were met at the other end of the journey and guided through the equatorial heat and chaos of city streets far from the propriety of Repulse Bay Road. Once at Jesse's house, there was again peace to be found in cool and flowered courtyards, long expanses of perfect wooden floors, and silent movement of family and staff alike.

As an only child of divorced parents, I was drawn to people who all sat down to a meal together and chatted about an ordinary day's events. That we were in the middle of Thailand in the home of a senior UN official mattered less to me than playing a role in a fifties sitcom. At that very first supper, there was talk, amongst other things, of in-country travel by train. But when I heard that an eighteen-hour journey on a hard bench was part of the deal, I immediately decided to stay behind and explore Bangkok, assured by the family that I would not be imposing. I actually liked the idea of continuing to be part of things.

Tom and Jesse left on the hard bench, and I quickly settled into a rhythm, taking buses and meeting up with various family members to sightsee, eat, or simply saunter. We played board games and bridge in the evenings and once went to the movies to see *Tora! Tora! Tora!*, the screen so crowded with multilingual subtitles—Chinese, Thai, Japanese, and English—that the images had become telescoped into its very center. The house eventually went quiet when Jesse's brother and sister left on holiday trips with their friends and my host departed on some diplomatic mission. By then, though, I already felt settled in the city, easily getting around town and back home for supper on my own.

Left alone with my hostess, I gradually became aware of familial imperfections, a veil lifting in the absence of other family members. We chatted at length, but I was simply unable to keep up with the drinking. Unaccustomed to an environment affected by alcohol, I was loathe to admit a problem, preferring to play my part in this black and white television program. When I finally excused myself to go to bed one evening, Jesse's mother and I left it that we would meet up in the morning and take in some special sites that she'd recommended over supper.

An early riser, I got up and ate breakfast on my own. With Tom and the family gone, the silence of the house was no surprise, with only the gliding servants and Jesse's mother left there with me. I then returned to a room no longer shared with a roommate. There I waited, reading my guidebook, until it was time to leave the house. After a good long while I finally ventured downstairs, hoping to get the show on the road. Jesse's mother was nowhere to be seen, nor were the servants able to explain her absence. I returned to my room, noting that the door to the master bedroom remained closed. Time passed and a maid appeared in my room to tidy up. By then, I had grown anxious, prompting me to take the maid by the arm to that closed door, and seek her support in silence as I turned the knob.

There we found her, sprawled across the bed, a bottle of empty pills at her side. Despite the absence of a common language, the maid knew to run for help and I knew that I needed to stay put and try to revive the unconscious lady. Although time seemed to slow unbearably, doctors were soon on the scene; and then I found myself going along in the ambulance, somehow understanding that this had not been the first time medics had been called out on such an emergency.

My next days were spent in the hospital, playing bridge with a woman back from the brink who acknowledged none of the drama in which we now found ourselves. That I quickly understood the need to maintain a charade only heightened my stress; thus, when Tom and Jesse reappeared on the scene, enlivened by their adventure, I was beside myself with eagerness to leave Bangkok. After all, I had been left alone in a troubled household, ignorant of its complexities, and ultimately obliged to grow too close to a situation that never should have come my way. Though Tom was initially bewildered by my brusque welcome upon his return, he quickly sympathized with my predicament.

I had casually noticed in the newspaper that Burma was issuing visas again, the country having been off limits to foreigners for several years. In the context of my reunion with Tom, during which I filled him in on what he had missed, I declared that I would be going to the Burmese Embassy the following day in the hopes of securing an immediate visa. Tom reacted by expressing regret that so swift a departure would deprive him of the opportunity to see some of Bangkok's highlights, hoping to stay on a few days to fill in the blanks. He quickly understood, though, that I needed to be away soonest and escape so troubling a domestic environment.

On the very next morning, Tom and I were at the embassy, a lovely place clearly unaccustomed to adventurers wanting to visit Burma. Confusion aside, we finally prevailed, leaving the embassy with fresh and valid stamps in our passports. From there, we went on to the Union of Burma Airways office and booked passage to Rangoon on the following day, assuming accommodations would not be a problem. Only the Strand was recommended, but the hotel was simply too pricey for our budget.

Rangoon came as a surprise with its King's English and colonial past; embedded within a decaying cityscape, it had long suffered from neglect and mismanagement. And then there were all those ladies puffing on enormous cigars! Through the streets, lined with elegant and multi-colored buildings in varying states of disrepair, we found our way to the Y, where we were welcomed by a bubbly and smarmy manager who immediately asked if we might have any ladies' cosmetics for sale. He hardly missed a beat when we disappointed him, writing out a list of what he needed and extorting a promise that we would send the requested cosmetics on to him as soon as we returned to America. As though in a trance, we agreed.

Aside from the Shwedagon Pagoda, I remember less the specific sights than fleeting images of Rangoon. It was thrilling to climb those marble steps to the top of this most sacred of stupas. We passed first through chaotic alleys of stalls and hawkers, emerging up into the holiness of the pagoda, which led me, swept up by the moment, to compare myself to a lotus, with my pure white petals managing to rise above the muddy waters. Monks wandering noisily about clad in saffron cloth quickly snapped me out of my sophomoric reverie, and I knew that, had I shared my thoughts with them, they would have fallen about in stitches.

Memories of Mandalay, our next stop, have been best forgotten by choice, though some just won't vanish: my covering a bed in shredded newspapers to avoid touching sheets crawling with live stock, and our witnessing a pack of goats devouring a pile of dead dogs (or was it the other way around?) right in the main street. One pleasurable image does survive—a dreamlike view from the hilltop overlooking the old colonial racecourse. Tom and I decided to cut our visit short and leave immediately for Pagan, the ancient capital.

There was a guest house on the banks of the Irrawaddy River, about which W. Somerset Maugham had written. It afforded us dramatic views of the landscape, dotted with dead-white stupas and reliquaries. We were free to roam and enter them; and once inside, high flying bats were our only company. While unable to recount too many details, I can honestly say that almost four decades later, the vision of those pristine and deteriorated holy places still occasionally come to mind as I fall asleep, all the more precious since a serious earthquake did significant damage in that very area a few years later.

There was nothing dream-like about our fellow guests. The hotel was packed with Russians who enthusiastically included us in their consumption of vodka, bottles of which kept magically appearing well into the night. They were also mighty keen to change money into dollars. Tom and I were clearly out of our depth, hoping that a cool facade would not betray our fear of somehow falling afoul of authorities in this military state.

When it came time to leave, our travel plans were mysteriously derailed, and we found ourselves bound for Rangoon on a slow train, a long bench our only seat. And then there was that single hole in the floor—the tracks literally whizzing beneath the squatter—at the end of the carriage. It was the only toilet available to us since the cars did not connect. The early stops along the way struck us with their charm. Because of the disconnect from one car to the next, the hawkers at each station had somehow to crawl in and out of windows, magically balancing their goods in order to pass amongst us, chanting "yam-i-yeh [sic];" and then there were those little old ladies on the platforms puffing on daunting cheroots and gossiping in terribly posh English accents. The novelty, though, soon wore off. The more stops we made, the harder the bench seemed to grow.

The twenty-four-hour trip on that train was punishing, but the familiarity of the Y swiftly revived us. We were shortly contacted by a UN official, Mr. P.K. Ghosh, alerted to our presence by Jesse's father who took us out to supper that very evening. Then, on the next day, the manager of the Y saw fit to introduce us to a Mr. A.T.C. Bone, a long time English expat and self-educated antiquarian. Mr. Bone, a charming caricature of an eccentric academic right out of a *Carry On* film, presented himself in our room at an appointed time. Even before greetings were exchanged, he sat down on the bed, peeled an orange and placed a piece of the skin in the keyhole. Tom and I were simply thrilled by such a display of intrigue in a country teeming with prohibition about trafficking in artifacts. Peel in place, Mr. Bone went on to unwrap some treasures for our perusal. While Tom agonized over provenance and price, I chose a small Buddha with a removable bodhi tree hinged to its back along with a terra cotta tile stamped with myriad images of the Buddha. By the time Tom had finished his transaction, I was long adrift in lore attending my treasures. Mr. Bone left, but not before stealthily removing the orange peel from the door. Several years later at my first teaching job in Oberlin, I opened *The New York Times* only to read an enormous obituary of A.T.C. Bone, the renowned expert on Burma.

The day of our purchases happened to coincide with my birthday; and much to my surprise, Tom offered to buy me a drink at the Strand. We entered a lobby of contrasts: an arrogant doorman in threadbare uniform, decrepit furniture with crisp antimacassars, and lifeless live music. We headed for the bar, excited by entering this transposed set of *Great Expectations*. Though the very grand room was empty, we were summarily halted at the entrance by a maître d' who gave us the once over. That I towered over him did not matter; I felt as if the haughty gentleman were peering down upon me.

"Are you guests in the hotel?" he stated more than queried.

When we said "No," he gleefully mentioned that without ties, we could not possibly be admitted. My ensuing charm offensive about birthdays, poor students, fans of Burma, etc., got us nowhere. Turned away, I took solace in the fact that a limousine would shortly be waiting for us at Kai Tak Airport in Hong Kong. Tom and I left the little man and went instead to have ice cream, but we never finished our cones—we were scared off when filthy glasses of water arrived.

I must have repacked my knapsack a dozen times for fear of customs discovering the treasures bought from Mr. Bone—but all for nothing as we were shooed on to the Union of Burma Airways plane. Despite the easy time on the way out, we somehow knew that none of the cosmetics requested by the manager of the Y would ever reach him from America, thereby justifying our decision not to do his bidding.

The Mercedes was, indeed, there for us, and we were immediately plunged into Chinese New Year celebrations once back at the house. The very day of our return, Mrs. Siu insisted that I accompany her to the annual flower market in Victoria Park. It is customary for Chinese homes to display blossoming branches during the holiday, which actually ushers in the spring. As we roamed amongst the aisles of forced flowers, I did not expect Mrs. Siu to hone in on a huge peach tree that she simply assumed I could handle for her. I suddenly knew why it was me, rather than diminutive Tom, who had been chosen for this outing. Back at the car, she was particularly pleased with the manner in which I maneuvered the tree across the two rear windows, new growth out one side and balled earth coming out the other. Over two decades later, as a Hong Kong resident myself, it was my pleasure to saunter through those very aisles, opting rather for the curious "five generations one home" stalks (*wudai tongtang*), with their gourd-like yellow protrusions resembling inflated surgical gloves.

At one of the many banquets that followed, I was seated next to an elderly lady. She was most patient with my feeble Mandarin, coaxing vocabulary out of me much like the kindest of language teachers. At one moment during our painful exchange I lapsed into English, expressing confusion because I mistakenly thought that she had asked me to visit her castle, if time permitted, prior to my return to Taiwan. She chuckled, first complimenting my comprehension, and then repeating the invitation in English.

Mrs. Yu turned out to be the last wife of a renowned Hong Kong figure, a native of Yunnan (the birth place of Dr. Siu, Annie's father) and a purveyor of herbs. He had in fact built two identical castles on Hong Kong Island—one on Blue Pool Road and another opposite the Repulse Bay Hotel known as Yu Cliff. I had passed the latter on several occasions wondering exactly what it was. With turrets, walls, balconies, and formal gardens, it was hard to miss, making little sense in this tropical colony.

It was shortly before our departure that Tom and I took Mrs. Yu up on her invitation and visited the castle, arriving at the end of an intricate drive whereupon we were greeted by liveried footmen and maids. And a palace it was, with rooms lined in exotic stone and walls sagging with massive tapestries, lit for a gala by gilded chandeliers. Although Mrs. Yu was in Blue Pool Road at the time, we were assured of her warm welcome and urged to explore the house and gardens at our leisure; and we did.

Not long thereafter, I was back on the mountainside, standing, once again, on the bare brick floor of a freezing dorm room. My spirits took a real dive as I unpacked and came upon that white suit, feeling not only as though I was back to square one, but had never even left, let alone danced a night away. But right at the very bottom of my bag, beneath the shorts and t-shirts, were my black shoes, the velvet bow tie flopping out of one of them, placed there for safe-keeping. I had been to the ball.

The Nurse in Kaifeng

There exists only one photograph of my paternal grandfather—a still made from a home movie, with him in top hat and formal wear. He was American born, unlike all my other grandparents, and of Hungarian stock, went to Cooper Union in New York City, died young, and was revered by his eldest son, my father—a man who admired no one.

From what I gather, there was simply no discussion about my name during my mother's pregnancy. It was to be Peter, for my father's father. After all, there would be no grandchildren from my father's brothers, Ruby and Bernard. The former had been shot down over Italy during the War, and the latter, completely incapacitated from birth by cerebral palsy. My mother had no problem with calling me Peter. Although she might have wanted her first child named for her mother, there would be many children born to her siblings who could easily honor their matriarch.

There was a problem, though, when it came to my middle name. My father also wanted me named for his late brother. Meaning no disrespect, my mother put her foot down, not because she was keeping score, but rather out of superstition. She was not about to name her firstborn after two men who had died so young. But, mindful of the unlikelihood that her late brother-in-law would ever have a namesake, she suggested that only his "R" be kept, thereby honoring his memory without burdening the baby with such unfortunate karma. Thus, I became Peter Rupert and not Peter Ruben.

Three decades later, I had the good fortune of making my first trip to China. The Cultural Revolution had just ended, and rare tours were tentatively venturing into a country long cut off from the outside world. These were the days before posh excursions catering to sniffy travelers. Rather, we were a random bunch of adventurers defying type who simply had to be in China.

On a long coach ride in the environs of Kaifeng (we were the first foreigners to visit this former capital and center of Jewish life in China), I was seated beside an enormous nurse. Despite all of our outings along the way, we had never been in each other's company. I had heard only that her suitcase was filled with special scotch that she was taking to some nuns in Hong Kong, where our tour would conclude.

We chatted leisurely on a bus wandering through a bleak winter landscape, and she mused at just how far away she felt from home. Anyone on that bus could have made the same comment, and I casually asked whence she had come. "Florida," she replied. After describing it as God's waiting room, I congratulated her on sitting next to a very rare breed—a native Floridian! We had a good laugh and began chatting about the state I had left at eight, occasioned by the divorce of my parents. There had obviously been tremendous change since my departure. The combination of desegregation and the Cuban diaspora had certainly transformed the sleepy, red-neck area of my early childhood beyond recognition—to be sure, "Dixie" was no longer sung each morning in the classroom.

My seatmate had just retired from a career in nursing and as though programmed to do so, she immediately took off to China, a place that had long obsessed her. Though she didn't like Chinese food, was disinterested in Chinese culture, and ill suited to travel—her girth made the simplest activities both awkward and exhausting—her place at my side made sense. I understood perfectly just how China can get you by the throat.

There we were, in the heartland of the Middle Kingdom, chatting away. Though decades and geography divided us, we quizzed each other about life in the Sunshine State. That I spoke Chinese interested her, and she recalled our guide putting me in my place on the airplane journey into China, warning me that he was in charge and that the expertise he brought to the table as a seasoned traveler was far more valuable than a bit of Chinese spoken by a school teacher from California. All I had done was offer to help people fill in their customs documents, as the English on the papers made no sense. But as events unfolded over the course of the trip, the guide grew completely dependent on me, his initial snub so redressed by deference that I came to resent the responsibility. Nonetheless, the nurse's sensitivity was most appreciated.

All of her working life had been spent in a hospital. She liked the structure, the sense of community. Her sexuality a puzzlement, I sensed her need somehow to belong. Hand-carrying bottles of scotch, obviously available in Hong Kong, further illustrated a desire to please. Such a public gesture, with its attendant hassles, gave the impression that she was happily obligated to and valued by her nuns.

A sense of inevitability prompted a question without thought.

"By any chance, did you ever work at St. Francis Memorial Hospital in Miami Beach?"

To her immediate affirmative response, I volunteered that I had been born in that hospital.

"Of all things, I was an obstetrical nurse!" she gushed.

We then chatted about dates.

"Nineteen forty-nine! I was working there in the delivery room. It's a shame that you don't know the name of your mother's obstetrician," she commented with disappointment.

"But I do."

Then and there, on the outskirts of Kaifeng, within sight of the Iron Pagoda, the tallest structure in the world when built during the Song Dynasty, I recounted the tale of my naming.

"... I became Peter Rupert—not Peter Ruben, and the name of my mother's doctor was Rupert Arnell."

"I was his nurse," she chuckled. "I guess we have no secrets, young Rupert."

China Bound

Clearly, my first discussion would have to be with Aunt Marcy. As my mother's guardian angel—though often portrayed as her warden—her elder sister would be asked to shoulder even more responsibility in my absence.

The call had come out of the blue.

"Mr. McGillicuddy would like to see you," was the polite request from our company chairman's own guardian angel and warden. An appointment was duly set up. Things were suddenly to change for me in the bank after that summons.

A week before the phone call, a delegation had arrived in New York City from the Bank of China, with Manufacturers Hanover Trust Company playing host at the Waldorf Suite. Paul, a pal of mine who worked on the China desk (though there was no China to cover in the early eighties) was scheduled to hold forth on letters of credit in Mandarin, but at the last moment, he walked away from the assignment, consumed by nerves and a most inappropriate crisis of confidence. Though working on Southeast Asian matters myself, I was drafted on the day before the event to step in, and the speech was dropped off at my apartment later that evening. I spent the whole night poring over dreaded simplified characters alluding to letters of credit, a far cry from either *The Analects of Confucius* or the local history of Yunnan in the Ming Dynasty, the texts with which I was most familiar from my education at Princeton in the East Asian Studies Department.

All I knew about the Waldorf Towers was that General Douglas MacArthur had lived there. Now, there I was, being ushered into the Manny Hanny suite, the sitting room set up with rows of chairs, occupied by attentive Chinese guests. The men were in blue suits, ditto for the ladies, and all were cradling identical plastic clutch bags bearing the logo of the Civil Aviation Authority of China (CAAC), China's national airline, in their laps. I was introduced by an un-known colleague in English, which was then interpreted by their Chinese minder. After all, these were early days, with the Cultural Revolution's pall still hanging low.

The details of my own performance are a blur. What I do recall is that by the end of the talk, my jacket was off and I was mopping my brow. Although he suspected all along that I was not, in fact, imparting the intricacies of letters of credit, the Chinese interpreter was gracious enough, as well as protocol savvy, not to interrupt and not to make it obvious that I was not being understood. When I did finally finish, a cheer filled the room; by then, our guests were all leaning forward in their chairs, as if coaxing the Chinese out of me. What the American senior bankers witnessed was a display of goodwill and relief amongst the Chinese rather than gratitude for revelations. Nonetheless, my career had been determined that afternoon.

Mr. McGillicuddy was legendary and the ebullient successor to Gabriel Hauge, a grand and dour Norwegian with a black eye patch.

Suddenly, I was in the chairman's office; a hand waving a cigar, more baton than tobacco, directed me to a seat. I remember thinking that Al Hirschfeld, the Broadway caricaturist of the continuing line, would have had a ball drawing Mr. McGillicuddy, and I wondered how the artist might have embedded the "Ninas" in the flailing arm that was orchestrating my audience. It was right out of a movie. I was being handled, and I loved it. Mr. McGillicuddy was a cross between tycoon, evangelist, and Tammany boss—completely irresistible.

"Heard about that performance of yours in the suite recently," he bellowed; "and I would have sweated like a pig as well." Then came the sound bites: "license approved in China;" "career opportunity;" "we're both Princetonians;" "one of the first American banks in Beijing;" "when can you leave?"

I was stunned by the opportunity. Having visited China in 1978—this was 1982—I reckoned it would be a good long while before my return. Now, I was being presented with the chance to live there, not as an academic hemmed in by some arcane topic of investigation, but rather as a pioneer at the very vanguard of America's foray into China, and right in the capital. He thought he had me, and I wanted to be had, but there was my mother's extremely poor health. With that, the robber baron became the village priest, lowering his voice, completely sharing in my predicament. Although he understood perfectly why I might be obliged to decline the posting, if I needed anything to make this work, I was to deal directly with him.

I had to speak to Aunt Marcy straightaway. When I returned to my desk in a daze, I was asked if I could attend some charity luncheon at which the bank had taken a few tables. As usual, senior bankers had backed out at the last moment, unleashing a three line whip to fill the seats. I simply shrugged off the request, too distracted by the prospect of a new life in China; but then an idea took hold.

Using the luncheon theme as a point of departure, I conjured up a charade that would afford me the opportunity to discuss China with my aunt. I would say I had been asked to attend an event with Leona Helmsley, the legendary wife of one of New York's great property developers, and I could bring a guest. Knowing full well that my mother was too unwell to attend, I also knew she would suggest that Aunt Marcy attend in her stead.

I made the call and all went according to plan. There I was, standing in front of the Four Seasons Restaurant the very next day, waiting for Aunt Marcy. She arrived, looking terribly elegant, this big lady (never fat in my family) whose girlish enthusiasm for adventure belied both her age and experience. She was clearly ready to rub elbows with Leona.

"There's been a change of plans," I offered sheepishly, leading the way to a restaurant right off of Park Avenue renowned for its spareribs and owned by a retired baseball player. (Despite her kosher home and traditional ways, she ate bacon, spareribs, and seafood at the drop of a hat.) My aunt was puzzled by our change of plans, but took my arm nonetheless and followed. Once seated, I began my story, concluding with the words, "You have veto power, Aunt Marcy."

Tears trickled down her cheek before another word was said. That she exercised her veto so swiftly came as a shock—so immediate and declarative from a woman who always found a way. It was my turn to make good on respect for her judgment. Nothing was going to change. My mother would remain exiled to Forest Hills in Aunt Marcy's permanent care, pining to return to her own apartment in Manhattan that I was now occupying. There would be no China for me.

The sudden intensity of a memory almost hurt. Right after Aunt Marcy had been widowed, I was sitting quietly with her in Forest Hills, the company finally gone and the mourning stools put aside.

"Uncle Dave must have loved me," she mused so softly that I'm not sure I was even meant to hear the words. "He didn't die in the house."

Uncle Dave had, in fact, collapsed in the street, dead of a heart attack even before he hit the ground; that this had happened, outside of the house and away from her, was the sign she had taken that he had in fact loved her. For almost five decades, theirs had been the stormiest of marriages, which included a separation so distant in the past that it was either unknown or forgotten by most of the family. It was often an ordeal to be with them, yet their patterns of behavior were so familiar that things could not have been otherwise. And in his mode of death, she recognized love.

Over the debris of spareribs, I gently suggested, "How about Mom coming back to Manhattan with a housekeeper to live with her full-time?"

We both tacitly understood that my mother would die in the not too distant future. I reckoned that if her end came in her own home, which she herself would value, my going to China might actually be a solution for these sisters rather than a problem for us all. Just as my aunt had equated love with being spared her husband's death at home, she realized that with my mother back in the City, death would again be at arm's length, somehow again demonstrating love. Her tears instantly vanished, and she quickly demanded the details of my chat with the chairman: What was office was like? Did he know you had been a teacher?....

Though the veto had been rescinded, I still had to discuss the opportunity with my mother. I took the next day off, having told her I needed to see her alone—a request that delighted her—and then took the E train to Forest Hills.

The door opened and there she stood, somehow again pulled up to her great height of five feet ten inches, looking more like the cross between Lauren Bacall and Simone Signoret of her youth than a withering victim of rheumatic heart disease, which had lurked since childhood.

She was positively statuesque as she offered her blessing to my adventure in a most breezy manner, her delivery completely divorced from the reality of the likelihood that my send-off to China would likely be our last time together. Aunt Marcy had done spadework, this was apparent; but the manner in which my mother handled the situation could only have been done by her. After I had recounted the details to her, she said simply and serenely, "There is really nothing to discuss," and sent me on my way, her grace never more radiant. My own relief and pleasure at the conclusion of the visit was so great that I paid no mind to the scene likely unfolding back in the apartment I had just left.

Between the time of my mother's blessing and my departure to China, there is little I recall. But what is lost to memory is made up by the events of my very last night in New York. Although it was my mother who had been the vortex of concern in the unfolding of this adventure, my father's last moment involvement makes for heady narrative.

Over the course of my life, my father had been an erratic figure. Married four times, this charismatic, brilliant self-saboteur had somehow made himself parentally available as I prepared to leave the country. I had actually asked him to come to New York from his home in Florida, my birthplace, to see me onto the plane. Though my parents had begun chatting during this preparatory period prior to my departure, I assumed that their shared lifetime of acrimony would prevail, preventing anything beyond the most cursory contact. This was not the case. My mother recounted a conversation with him during which she had reflected that no matter what had happened between them, she would always be grateful to him—for me; and in that spirit, she invited him to supper on my last evening in Manhattan.

Annette, now installed as my mother's housekeeper, had been given the night off but a fine supper had still been prepared. There we sat, our nuclear family together for the first time since my childhood; and there they sat, that once stunning couple, chatting away, almost in code, about things I little understood. As the evening unfolded, my mother insisted upon being very much the hostess, summoning all of her meager strength and transforming it into full-fledged energy. My parents sat together on the sofa, involved in a way that would have seemed rather natural had I grown up in such company.

It was time to make my way to the Waldorf, where the bank had provided a room as a parting gesture, and I left them. As I walked eastward from the Parc Vendome on West 56th Street, I looked up and caught sight of the very top of the AT&T building's skeleton, a gossamer breakfront whose place in the skyline announced post-modernism with a vengeance. I noticed it once again en route to the 59th Street Bridge the following crisp December morning on my way to the airport. My adventure in China was about to begin.

In early spring, when the annual dust storms remind residents of Beijing just how close we are to the Gobi Desert, I called my mother to wish her a happy Passover. I knew she would unlikely be able to celebrate the holiday with Aunt Marcy. Quite frankly, she preferred staying put in Manhattan under any circumstances. She, of course, wanted details of my new life, mentioning that she had seen me interviewed in front of the Jianguo Hotel where I both lived and worked. I liked the idea that the locale was visibly known to her, making our chat somehow more real. Embellishing was easier than defining, and she could not hear enough. My mother then began updating me on life in New York, her voice belying neither illness nor confinement. She mischievously confessed to eating a bowl of pasta on Passover, swearing me to secrecy. "Don't tell Aunt Marcy," she giggled. She then spoke of a recent outing that had taken them both to the Upper West Side. A friend was doing a one-woman tribute to Anna Russell, and they wanted to demonstrate their support for her. Her account trailed off with the words, "...and if that didn't kill me...."

The call came the very next night. My mother was dead.

The Rectification of a Name

We were all under Madam Bai Shizhen's thumb. With her "bowl on the head" haircut, blue Mao suit, and national health glasses, she gave little away except the gravity with which she discharged her responsibility for foreign bankers in the Beijing of 1982. For domiciled foreigners in post-Cultural Revolution China, that brand of responsibility was tricky, indeed. None of us could really fathom the horrors of that epoch, let alone comprehend a local getting carted off for simply wearing a German watch.

I had first visited China in 1978 on a tour with family. Coming back to live in Beijing now was simply thrilling! I had been chosen as the Manufacturers Hanover Trust Company's founding representative, reporting to Tim Weitzer, a legendary China hand based in Hong Kong. He was said to have been an Air America pilot during the Vietnam War, and he had the whiff of a spy about him. A volatile fundamentalist Christian who knew his way around China, getting the bank onto the mainland was clearly his baby.

Having learned that the bank's application had been approved, Tim and I traveled up to Beijing to receive the appropriate official documents. In that spirit, we presented ourselves at the old Bank of China building right off of Tiananmen Square. Madam Bai and a greasy-haired flunky welcomed us—a quarter century later, he is a big wig in one of the state banks. (When we meet up these days, he talks about our good old times that certainly escape my memory.) There was a third person in that room, as well. His name was Pu

Dacheng, and he was clearly of mixed Chinese ancestry. Madam Bai immediately let us know that he was now assigned to us as our primary contact within the Bank of China. His leathery hand stunned me when I shook it. Only the punishing experience of having been "sent down" to hard labor in the countryside could have accounted for such texture. Mr. Pu knew some English, taught to him by his American mother who married his Chinese father as a student abroad; and that must have accounted for his recall to the capital in order to assist the bank in rejoining the world. But his mixed parentage had also ensured particularly brutal treatment during the Cultural Revolution. As stern as he tried to be, he simply could not hide a liveliness that went on to inform our relationship during my sojourn in Beijing. Years later, news of his subsequent suicide hit me hard.

Once introductions were out of the way, tea had been sipped, and small talk had become too little to matter, Madam Bai suddenly stood up and announced that our license had been approved. She ceremoniously handed Tim Weitzer assorted papers sporting myriad red seals. There was a real sense of moment owing to the rarity of lawfully licensed foreign firms in China. I began babbling away in Chinese, peppered by expressions probably best understood by Madam Bai's parents—the Cultural Revolution had removed much color from the language. Such linguistic touches, courtesy of having studied classical Chinese in Taiwan, at Princeton, and at Middlebury, provided much amusement. Then, it all ended. Tim withdrew his hand from the shakes and abruptly asked Madam Bai about the Chinese name given to the bank. It was not the one he had requested. She responded that in the Bank of China's files,

Manufacturers Hanover Trust Company was always known as Hannowei Bank. He simply returned the documents and bade farewell. Slack-jawed, I followed in silence.

Tim's Christianity certainly did not inform his vocabulary. The expletives came thick and fast as we walked purposefully to the car that would take us to our next call. It was to see Mr. Hong Min, a senior official involved in the oversight of the Bank of China's relations with international financial institutions. A short drive away, we were soon at yet another decrepit building, warmly welcomed as more lidded teacups were filled before us. Though the scene was familiar, I was immediately confused. In response to Mr. Hong's inquiry about how things had been going for us, Tim was positively benign, expressing gratitude for our approval and heaping praise on Madam Bai. The two men then simultaneously grabbed for their tea cups, staring at each other over the rising steam.

When the cups were finally lowered, Tim breezily recounted a bit of a misunderstanding that morning. Somehow, Madam Bai had gotten it wrong, leading her to bestow the wrong Chinese name on the bank. After all, the name we wanted, Hanhua, was a splendid double evocation of China to which there could be no objections. He then asked for the grandee's advice. Without hesitating for a moment, Mr. Hong leapt to his feet and left the room. Tim immediately put his finger to his lips, suggesting that we could somehow be overheard. In a flash, Mr. Hong was back, with a broad smile on his face. Teacups were lifted again, but our host lowered his quickly, telling us that we were expected by Madam Bai the next morning at ten o'clock. At that appointed time, twenty-four hours after our initial appearance in her office, we received our documents—with the name Tim requested. I have always wondered if Mr. Hong had already spoken to Madam Bai by the time we had arrived to see him. Whatever the sequence and details of events, an unacceptable situation had been avoided: an unclaimed permit for a foreign bank to open in China under a name it did not recognize.

Shortly after participating in this shadow play, I made my permanent move to China, living and working in the Jianguo Hotel. The hotel was a copy of a Palo Alto Holiday Inn—a glorified motel in California, but cutting edge in China—and it was the talk of Beijing: China's first joint venture hotel with foreign management and potable water. There was little time to enjoy its amenities, though, with much to be done in preparation for the opening festivities. With John F. McGillicuddy, the bank's frisky chairman, arriving shortly to host events, I somehow knew that my future was inextricably linked to their precision.

In the midst of all this activity, someone happened to ask about our advertisement. As a matter of course, the Chinese authorities simply expected that our opening would be marked in print. I had seen no reason to ply our wares in the bizarrely-colored magazines aimed at the foreigners, nor was I in a position to deal with the foreign press. That left *The People's Daily*, with no bigger bang for the buck. I quickly gathered some photos for a layout, including one of a 747 to highlight our involvement in China's very first airplane lease; there was also one of Mr. McGillicuddy along with senior officials he had met on a previous visit. Chosen with great care, I ensured that no one in the shot had been purged. I also wrote the copy and worked with a wordsmith from *The People's Daily* to get things just right. Once completed, the package was sent off to Madam Bai for her imprimatur; and then came the phone call. It was Madam Cao Xiaoxing, the jolliest of Madam Bai's sidekicks. Her Gatling gun delivery of Shanghainese-accented Mandarin simply daunted me. The details were difficult: in two days, I was to show up at Madam Bai's office at either ten o'clock or four o'clock (the pronunciations of "ten" and "four" can be perilously similar in various dialects); but there was nothing unclear in the message itself. Madam Bai had a problem with the advertisement.

I did not take my bicycle on the call, preferring the shabby gravitas of my state-supplied black Russian car. We circled Tiananmen en route to the old Bank of China building to its west, the scene of that initial drama over our name. These were the years sandwiched between the Cultural Revolution and the Massacre, and the square, once covered in ancient buildings and trees, was a desolate and artificial space. Created by Mao after Liberation in 1949, it aped Red Square and was used for state-sponsored and staged demonstrations. During the Cultural Revolution, it became Mao's launching pad for attacks on the very state which he had created. With his power seeping away, and identifying with a dead parent at his own funeral, he loosed forces on society from which China is still recovering. This deadly space, so closely associated with frenzy and tragedy, can falsely lead one to believe that Beijing has no heart.

In the dead of winter, it was so cold in the Bank of China building that guests not only wore hats and coats, but grew accustomed to seeing their breath, as well. The uninitiated might marvel at the heartiness of their Chinese hosts in simple Mao suits. What was not seen, though, were the layers of long underwear into which locals seemed to be sewn starting on a certain date, and from which they did not emerge until another.

I did show up at the wrong time, though I was made to cool my heels (literally) before being sent on my way. Told to return at four, I arrived promptly and was immediately ushered into Madam Bai's office, its peeling paint and water-stained walls in no way diminishing her stature. There she stood, behind her desk, arms crossed, ready to pounce; and she did!

"You know that First Chicago was the first American bank in China. How dare you claim it was Manny Hanny in your proposed ad!"

I meekly asked if I could be seated, a request that somehow altered her fury and introduced a sense of slow motion to our encounter.

"My advertisement says that we have full correspondent banking relations with all provinces of China, Madam Bai," I purred.

Though she agreed, her hand slashed the air, impatiently directing me to get on with things, anxious to see where I was going with all this.

"Is Taiwan part of China, Madam Bai?" I playfully queried.

Her patience clearly exhausted, the furious nod of her head was as good as a bark.

"It was my impression that First Chicago had to shut down in Taiwan for the privilege of opening on the Mainland, Madam Bai; thus, First Chicago does not have full correspondent banking relations with all provinces of China."

She slowly seated herself, her rage mounting on the way down. The more intense her gaze, the more my eyes wandered about the room. We then sat in silence.

"Xiao Li [the familiar diminutive of my name], this advertisement needs some work," Madam Bai pronounced, her monotone maintaining authority while steering towards compromise.

The ad did get published on time, with Manufacturers Hanover described as one of the first American banks in China. That neither Manny Hanny nor First Chicago exist today is a mere footnote to banking history; that both are now part of J.P. Morgan, a real twist. By the way, the advertisement, which appeared all over China, did bear fruit. Several weeks after its publication, a hulking man who I could smell before I could see, arrived in my office. He stood in the doorway, in a worn blue peasant suit, cap pulled way down on his head. Offering him cigarettes, a Coca Cola and a seat, I began the usual ballet of discovery, trying to find out what the gentleman really wanted.

"Milking machines. Your name in *The People's Daily* said that you were manufacturers; and in the steppe, they will make all the difference. When can you deliver them?"

Fowl Play

I had not been in China long. The team consisted of just me, my assistant Lucy, and our driver Mr. Qi (known as Xiao Qi or "Little" Qi, an appropriate and inoffensive diminutive); and we sat cheek by jowl in an office that was actually a small hotel room, barely emptied of the stacked mattresses that had cluttered it when my key first went into the lock.

This was Beijing in the winter of 1982, a bone dry, frigid, and windy capital still emerging from the Cultural Revolution, a combination that made settling in all the more difficult. Friendships with local folks were simply not possible owing to the peril still associated with foreigners. Well-intended liberals never understood that their pursuit of locals could actually endanger the very people they sought to embrace. There was neither a skyline nor fresh fruits and vegetables, with the roofs of low-slung houses still covered by white cabbages, the only locally grown vegetable available throughout the winter— constantly turned to guard against decay.

I had hired Lucy upon my arrival, realizing just how daunting my first chore was to be. The arrangement of opening festivities, to be attended by our chairman and almost seven hundred guests, was going to be an organizational nightmare. The bevy of expat Hong Kong cha-cha queens, knowing nothing of northern ways, got short shrift as they lined up for consideration. That they neither spoke Mandarin nor had connections (*guanxi*) about town convinced me that what I really needed was a seasoned local "dragon" to get the job done.

Lucy's name was in the ether. She had a long career at the American Consulate in Hong Kong, where her claim to fame was significant involvement in the Kissinger disinformation exercise attending his earliest trips into China. Lucy was part of the cabal that had convinced the world that the statesman was bound for Pakistan; and after she retired, she decided to return to her native Beijing, working on start-up operations in an environment more akin to the Wild West than the Middle Kingdom. I was told that she had recently left Marc Rich's famous trading company because of her objections to his sharp practices.

She agreed to see me, arriving in the lobby of the Jianguo Hotel, where I was both living and working, in a mink coat, traditional Chinese dress (*qipao*), and diamond earrings—a most regal lady, radiating a great sense of purpose; and the interview proceeded—she of me! Two things quickly became apparent: she was the person to get the job done, and I would be working for her.

Once terms were agreed, our rhythm of work became crisp and urgent. There was nothing standard in China at that time, so each endeavor was new. That I wanted lion dancers who would move amongst the tables (a highly controversial request since performers were meant to be confined to the stage) added to the complexity of the task. Nonetheless, with the help of our newly hired driver, Xiao Qi, himself a Chinese version of the artful dodger, we pushed ahead. There were moments of repose, though, and during some of them,

Lucy parceled out details of her past: an educated family, flight from the communists, a failed marriage to a Flying Tiger pilot, retreat along the Burma road, estrangement from her daughter, siblings' suffering during the Cultural Revolution. Such events actually traced the traumas of modern Chinese history; yet, the person recounting them proved far more complex than even her own story. The years I went on to share professionally with Lucy never seemed to build upon an evolving relationship. Rather, I felt newly introduced to her each day, never knowing which bit of her past would inform the present. Only her ability remained constant.

Nearing year-end, she suddenly invited me to accompany her to her nephew's home for lunch on New Year's Day. I was surprised for various reasons. By extending such an invitation, Lucy was blurring one of many fierce divides that compartmentalized her life. Furthermore, there was a recklessness about the invitation as the notion of a foreigner visiting a private home was still unusual.

I knew that her nephew, Ruan Ti, and his wife were both faculty members at Qinghua University, a most distinguished institution closely associated with the sciences. They had been abroad as well, and he was the son of Lucy's brother who lived in Suzhou, an elderly gentleman of distinction who had suffered bitterly during the Cultural Revolution. This complex story was reduced in my mind to a quandary over what gift I should bring my hosts. I could either buy them a necessity that was still considered a luxury—like good cooking oil—or simply a luxury, like candy. But even so pedestrian a choice was not simple.

At this time, there were two kinds of money: one for locals and one for foreigners. It was only with the latter that purchases could be made in the Friendship Store where "luxuries" were available. My pockets bulging with *waihui zhuan'r* (that hard "r" added so distinctively by Beijing folks), I walked there, westward against the wind along Chang'an Boulevard, the road that eventually passes between the Forbidden City and Tiananmen. As a foreigner, I strolled invisibly into the shop; but not so for the Chinese people who had to produce myriad cards covered in red seals in order to enter.

I had often been here, but usually in search of calligraphy brushes or antique oddities. On one occasion, when the weather suddenly turned cold, I was forced to buy a bright green down coat that almost fit. Despite the gap between the bottom of the sleeves and the tops of my gloves, it was the best I could find. The glee with which this sale had been made—of this lone and loud coat—led me to believe that the parka had been hanging around for a mighty long while. Now shopping for my New Year's hosts, I found myself wandering alone amongst electric fans and cookers, on the lookout for cooking oil. When I finally did find it, there were lots of Chinese milling around, examining the various containers with earnest care. These were largely older people, shuffling from shelf to shelf in cloth shoes and thread bare Mao suits, their shabby appearances at odds with the very notion of privilege that had secured their admission into the shop in the very first place.

I left abruptly. After all, what did I know about cooking oil? But then I realized that my haste had been truly prompted by profound discomfort. The way the bottles were being examined, I could have been in Tiffany's, and I reckon that in past lives, some of these people had been. I began imagining the individual dramas through which each had lived during the Cultural Revolution, "rusticated" to mean corners across the land to be taught bogus lessons born of power struggles fought to the death by Chairman Mao against his opponents. These oil shoppers were now being brought back from the pale, not out of charity, but necessity. With their juniors left uneducated during the decade of upheaval (1966-1976), they needed to tend to China's present if there was to be a future.

Back at the Jianguo Hotel, I bought a box of fancy imported chocolate in the near-empty lobby shop. Though the candy was a somehow wildly inappropriate gift, I knew it was just right. Considering Lucy's pedigree and the experiences of her relatives, they had to have known such things. Thus, my gift might just tap into memories rather than simply be something with no context of reference. It had not only been comical, but sad to see a senior Chinese official at a dinner hosted by President Reagan balancing fish mousse on a knife. I had confidence that my hosts would cope.

On New Year's Day of 1983, Xiao Qi drove us to the luncheon party. He, too, had of course been invited, though I was still adrift when it came to etiquette involving drivers. I knew that Lucy had hired Xiao Qi for his street smarts, all the while lamenting the fact that he had been deprived of an education; but, she could also be terribly haughty in his direction, making his presence at so personal an event not the most obvious of things to expect. Yet he simply had to be there. A bit of context: it was not possible to hire locals directly to work for a foreign firm. Thus, Xiao Qi had been hired through a government agency known as FESCO, which supplied all personnel. It was also well known that such people performed two jobs: providing services to employers and supplying information back to their *danwei*, the work unit to which they were primarily attached. In essence, the very personal and sensitive nature of Lucy's taking me to her relatives' home dictated that Xiao Qi be with us. In this way, the openness of it all robbed the occasion of any drama, thereby ensuring that we could all just have a good time.

That Xiao Qi and I have now been friends for decades sits awkwardly with my recollections of these early days. Owing to intimacy with foreigners, drivers were afforded recognition within the system enabling them to tyrannize—a power more often exercised against the local elite than against foreigners themselves. Many a posh banquet had been halted by a surly chauffeur who would sidle up to a senior Chinese and report that the prearranged food, beer, and cigarette allowances were simply inadequate. A cryptic and embarrassing huddle would then ensue, while the ignorant foreigners just hoped that those quotas would be swiftly hiked so the main event might continue. I came to realize that such encounters actually represented the institutionalization of hush money, paid to a lost generation which might well grow disgruntled enough to threaten the elite who were merely suffering the occasional indignities of loosening the purse strings.

Whatever awkwardness the charade might cause foreigners, the inevitable capitulation was a small price to pay for relatively cheap peace. Though Xiao Qi had shown himself to be an occasional banquet thug, he grew to become my closest friend in China.

Our black Russian car pulled up to a bleak cement block of flats within the grounds of the university. The combination of burning coal and loess, that ever present and distinct dust blown eastward from the Gobi Desert which manages to find every cranny in Beijing, blurred and soiled any trace of beauty to be found on the grim scene. We entered through doors ajar, with panes of glass either cracked or missing, and the halls, with stairs of concrete, even colder than the street and littered with aged rubbish. When the family's door opened, Lucy's nephew haltingly introduced himself to me as Tommy, immediately setting the tone for New Year's Day. This was not an occasion for me to be clever in Chinese, but one for letting a bit of the world back into life here in Tommy's China. He and his wife graciously accepted the box of Belgian chocolates in a most familiar and un-Chinese fashion. They casually placed it on a nearby folding table, suggesting that we might all enjoy a treat for dessert. In my view, dessert is *the* failure in Chinese cuisine, otherwise my favorite in the world. The suggestion of a sweet after the meal not only proved surprising, but was indicative of lingering memories of time spent abroad as a student and young professional.

The pleasure of just being in a home obliterated the meanness of its innards. That the interior differed little from the hall mattered not at all. Though fortunate to live in so posh a hotel, it was magic for me simply to be in a place with a kitchen. There were good smells as we ambled toward that folding table where the chocolates had been placed. In the dead of a Beijing winter, there was little reason to expect fine fare. After all, only food found locally was available to eat. Somehow, though, eating in a home transformed the occasion into something more special than it seemed. As we passed the afternoon, the usual pile of grizzle and bones grew alongside our bowls, with lively conversation in Chinese and English only adding to the warmth of the occasion. Xiao Qi was in fine form too, his role as spy co-opted by his inclusion in the jolly party.

Near the end of the meal, I needed to use the bathroom—little wonder after drinking so much hot tea. Much to my surprise, Tommy indicated the way to one within their own flat, not shared with neighbors. It was unbearably cold (and only years later, as I took a break from a Thanksgiving dinner in London, was I ever as cold as during that slash in Beijing). Temperature aside, I went about my business; and while looking lazily out at the bare trees of the Qinghua campus through the sooty window, a clucking chicken suddenly appeared from behind the toilet! I was so startled that my trousers and the floor ended up soaked. As I struggled silently and swiftly to clean up, using as little paper as possible, I noticed a straw-lined bushel wedged in behind the commode holding a few eggs.

The place again dry—though not me—and the chicken back in its basket, I returned to the table, my coat wrapped around me, welcomed back by straight faces and an offer of a truffle.

Dr. Fang's House Call

It bothered Lucy that I had no hair, and when my fierce assistant—an aging Beijing local who had returned to China after a lifetime abroad—honed in on something, it was only a matter of time before the issue was addressed to her satisfaction.

The mailman showed up in the office, Room 114 in the Jianguo Hotel, down a winding and narrow corridor dubbed "Wall Street" in the Beijing of the early eighties. Usually he'd simply hand over a packet of post and ask for *ba mao*, equal to eighty Chinese cents, for the "inspection" fee, which was shorthand for the money foreigners had to pay for the privilege of having our mail read. The routine was so predictable that the chap became known as Ba Mao Xiansheng—Mr. Eighty Cents—but today was different. There was a delivery waiting in the hall, and he needed some help. Mr. Qi, our canny driver who had been derailed by the Cultural Revolution and robbed of an education, jumped up and followed Mr. Eighty Cents out the door.

In short order, they were back. The dollies they were pushing appeared robotic, with each chap hidden behind boxes stacked so high that their faces were covered. The crates were unloaded in the middle of the office. With that, Mr. Eighty Cents handed over the more conventional correspondence, asking, as though for the very first time, for eighty cents. But, it was Mr. Qi, not Lucy, who handled this transaction. For some reason, the "Dragon" remained seated until the mailman left. In silence, she walked over to the cartons and opened one with a sharp blade. From within, she took out something

59

that looked like an egg box; but when the lid was lifted, tidy rows of ping-pong balls were revealed inside. Still in silence, she filled a tea mug with boiling water, poured from one of those ubiquitous flowery thermoses, removed one of the ping-pong balls, peeled a waxen cover off of it revealing a black sphere, and dropped it in the cup. She then told me to sit down at my desk and drink up after the brew had cooled. In the interim, Mr. Qi had found an envelope within the carton and opened it. He then appeared over me, holding a nasty looking wand, with many little spikes jutting out of one end of it.

Sensing my confusion and growing impatience, Lucy announced that she had ordered medicine from Anhui province that was guaranteed to grow hair. The studded mallet was needed to stimulate blood flow in my scalp. There I sat at my desk, the "Do Not Spit" sign from the Star Ferry in Hong Kong hanging behind me, sipping a bitter potion as Mr. Qi pounded my pate. Lucy was soon back on the telephone, leaving the hazing to the driver. From then on, the routine was repeated three times a day, and the six-month supply of bitter ping-pong balls that arrived on the robotic dollies ensured I would be committed to this program for the foreseeable future. Treated like a patient, I was callously subjected to random examinations by Lucy and Mr. Qi, who would debate the state of my hair growth as though I were not even present. There was no point in resisting.

Out on a call one day, I was picked up by Mr. Qi. He took me back to the hotel, the site of both my home and office—in the early 1980s, most foreigners were not permitted to rent flats, a luxury left only to diplomats, journalists, and airline employees. There was a hallway to the left of the reception desk in the lobby leading to my office, room

114, in "Wall Street," where some bank and commercial offices were located. (Neighbors of mine included Sandy Randt, who then worked for the nascent American Commercial Service and now serves as the ambassador to China, and Michael Langley, who had worked for HSBC in Shanghai in the late forties and was now, over four decades later, spearheading their return to China. A delightful gent with a wealth of pre-revolutionary tales, he was also ever the bar-fly, with a drink actually named after him in the hotel's watering hole.) Just before passing the front desk, I was stopped by a room boy who told me that I had guests waiting for me at a table near the piano.

There, an elderly man sat in worn and dusty cloth shoes and a Mao suit. His gray hair stood on end and tape held one arm of his spectacles in place. Fidgeting next to him was a little girl he proudly introduced as his granddaughter. I was warmly greeted by them both as they stood near me, all of us awkwardly milling about. Finally suggesting that we make our way back to my office, I found myself nervously babbling with complete strangers. I immediately offered the gentleman foreign cigarettes and the little girl a coke, a luxury that she found nothing short of thrilling. We chatted about my Chinese, his height—rather tall, her hair bows, hot running water in the hotel—potable, too… Growing desperate at such chit-chat with someone unknown to me, I was all the more startled by his command—both sudden and familiar—to be seated at my desk. Topping that, he began examining my head, commenting on healthy sprouts of hair on my shining crown. Lucy entered into this scene, immediately giving Dr. Fang from Anhui a spirited greeting, expressing surprise at his early arrival for his appointment with me. She joined Dr. Fang over my head, testifying to the change that had taken place since I had begun the daily regimen of medicine and massage. Before he and his granddaughter went on their way, the little girl laden with souvenirs, I had somehow ordered another six month supply of ping-pong balls, with a new mallet thrown in.

I remain bald.

Dumplings Al Fresco

Chinese folks eat so early, and they just don't eat outside. Spring came, and the days were growing longer; and I just could not face more ersatz Western food in overstuffed surroundings or another joint where you had to dip a plastic mug into a tub for some warm, flat, mystery beer to wash down some equally mysterious Chinese food. Wes, my guest from Texas, was unlike the usual visitors from abroad who, no matter how well traveled they might have been, became child-like in China, falling into my arms whether they knew me or not. He was low-maintenance and happy to get with any program.

Ritan (Altar of the Sun) Park was within striking distance of the Jianguo Hotel where I lived and worked. Although it wasn't ideal—I couldn't boil an egg for three years—it was considered the height of luxury; and I quickly learned that to berate it in the presence of locals was deeply insensitive, considering the deprivations of their daily lives. I considered its lobby my personal sitting room, and had grown used to seeing the likes of Elton John sporting a blond wig while playing the piano, Omar Sharif enjoying a rubber of bridge, and an Australian prime minister receiving Zhao Ziyang, the premier later purged in the aftermath of the Tiananmen Massacre. It was from here that Wes and I set out for the derelict temple in the park that served dumplings in its courtyard. We struggled through the rows of bicycles that baffled our exit from the rear of the hotel, finally able to stroll along the lanes, the spring dust giving way to the greenery of gnarled trees.

Going down Guanghua Road, I pointed out various embassies, their entrances crowded with gaudy displays of potted flowers—as though in competition with each other—and largely known to me from drinks parties held on Friday evenings on a rotating basis. Though not a "happy hour" type myself, there were few watering holes in this burg, and thus, I was occasionally tempted to show up. The British were particularly hospitable, opening up The Bell to the foreign community, a pub in the forecourt of the embassy, where the Chinese were, of course, excluded by their own authorities. At one of these occasions, I spotted a macho marine wearing a tee shirt advertising The Hobbit, a gay bar in Manila which specialized in dwarfs and their admirers. Overtaken by mischief, I sidled up to him and expressed my regret at being so tall. On we walked, eventually reaching the gate of the park where we had to make a payment—the only time coins ever changed hands because their value was so tiny they had no place in regular transactions—to gain admission. Winding amidst untidy foliage, random piles of paving stones, dog-eared posters lionizing the revolution and elderly spitters, we finally came upon the restaurant.

Chinese tables are infuriating. Whether made in the Ming Dynasty or yesterday, they invariably have a rail running all around them, below the top, making it simply impossible for a tall person to place legs comfortably beneath them. The greasy plastic cover hiding the rail ensured a bruised knee—fooled, yet again. But, once wedged in place, nothing could diminish the pleasure of dumplings *al fresco*.

We were the last ones out the door, the peeling red slab literally closing behind us most unceremoniously; and it wasn't even getting dark yet. As we began retracing our steps, I started to feel unwell almost immediately. Without wanting to draw attention to my worsening situation, I picked up the pace of our stroll, continuing on with the small talk. Not a moment later, Wes blurted out that he, too, needed to walk quickly. We looked at each other, both of us already broken out in that particular brand of sweat that means only one thing.

"There's no way we're going to make it back to the hotel; but there's no way we're using the public toilet either," I declared as we speed-walked out of the park. To this day, the mere prospect of a Chinese toilet still conjures up Fernando Rey's suicide in Lina Wertmüller's *Seven Beauties*. It was an experience to be avoided at all costs, and as I struggled to repress the memories of fumes and filth, I suddenly remembered The Bell, midway between the park and the Jianguo. Discomfort mounting by the step, I began instructing Wes.

"We're going to the British Embassy. There's a bar on the grounds, and we'll be able to use its bathroom. What you must do, though, is look straight ahead as we approach the gates. All Chinese security is directed against Chinese people so the guards will simply assume we belong if we look like we belong. No eye contact! Just walk straight through."

And we did successfully gain entry only to find The Bell locked tight. Now in dire straits, I knew there was not enough time to escape the compound and go elsewhere. There was still the residence, though. Having been there on a few occasions, I did recall several bathrooms right inside the front doors.

In we walked, immediately scattering like roaches at the flick of the kitchen light. After a short while, we regrouped in the front foyer and walked leisurely towards each other, any hint of urgency absent from our respective shuffles. Dusk finally upon us and our brows now dry, we then enjoyed our stroll back to the Jianguo.

A quarter of a century later, on income tax day, now an Anglo-American myself, I had the pleasure of returning to that embassy—this time by invitation of the ambassador, Sir William Ehrman, another eighties veteran—for supper with the Chancellor, Alistair Darling. Entry was like boarding a flight—security doors, metal detectors, the disgorging of BlackBerrys and money clips, and body searches with electronic wands.

Wes and I would have been in big trouble.

Detour to Bun Town

The forms were, indeed, intimidating, and stories of Beijing airport martinets only enhanced the peril of it all. The tale goes that when Mr. Gabriel Hauge, the formidable chairman of Manufacturers Hanover Trust Company, made his first trip to China in the seventies as part of a high profile delegation, he was asked to lift his eye patch for inspection by a customs officer.

When I took up residence just a few years later—inconceivable when Mr. Hauge had first visited during the Cultural Revolution—I came to know that those forms had to be done according to Chinese Hoyle, with specific goods being brought into the country and presented for inspection in a specific fashion. As a rare holder of a residency visa, I enjoyed being rather nonchalant about what others found traumatic. That being said, I was more than happy to assist the terrified.

Being six feet five inches tall, I always sat on the aisle, leaving the window seat to little folks. With a Trollope novel in hand, I immediately lost myself in nineteenth century English parish intrigues, an imaginary environment that I came to value all the more as the claustrophobia of life in Beijing grew more intense. Suddenly, though, I became aware of a rather compact fellow standing over me. Sporting a pinched and striped three-piece suit with a heavy peppering of dandruff, he could only have been an Englishman. That Hong Kong was still a colony might have minimized the contrast on the Peak, but on board a brand new and already dog-eared CAAC plane, with stewardesses sporting pigtails and the seats bedecked in socialist antimacassars, he could not have been a more striking innocent abroad, embodying arrogance and uncertainty rolled into one.

Clearly, he was anxious. Downing the novel in aid of my distressed companion, I began customary assurances. I was used to this routine as a somewhat smug China hand. As usual though, it was the Chinese themselves, the very source of the discomfort, who began to transform the situation into a comedy. To be sure, the meager gray cold cuts summarily served were no laughing matter, but a stewardess busily handing out nail clippers or kitsch picture frames as though these souvenirs made perfect sense was initially more surprising than amusing to the traveler, hinting at the new world about to be entered.

The trip was going well. The English gentleman had been a Gurkha and spoke Nepalese. After leaving the army, he joined a medical supply company, and this was to be its first foray into China, flogging anesthetics well outside the comfort of the Raj. He had some pals in the British Embassy who had paved his way, though these were not the best connections at the time. Negotiations were well underway over the future of Hong Kong. Mrs. Thatcher had recently visited Beijing, signed the Sino-British Joint Declaration, fallen down the front steps of the Great Hall of the People, and left the debris to her resident diplomats. But rather than hold forth on the current British predicament, I dwelled instead on The Bell, the pub within the embassy's grounds, and my close friendships with some of his compatriots.

I was savoring my role as in-flight raconteur, and apparently pleasing my travel companion, as well. But we did seem to be landing a bit soon, I thought. It was hard to tell, though, since there were virtually no skylines in the China of the early eighties, save Shanghai. The cities were still flat and sprawling, with little to recognize in the dark. Only when we were well on the runway was my suspicion confirmed. We were in Tianjin, a virtual hop from Beijing. A city once carved up by foreigners, it was a mini-version of Shanghai, with decaying noble architecture still redolent of bygone days; but it was foremost the home of the legendary *gou buli* buns. The story goes that a child nicknamed Puppy (*gouzi*) grew up to own a meat bun store. He was so intense about his cooking that he took no notice (*buli)* of anything but his buns. Thus, *gou buli*.

I casually mentioned to my neighbor that we had landed in Tianjin, instantly making light of the situation before he had the chance to panic. While not terribly concerned about the detour, I certainly was curious. We deplaned in complete ignorance and were politely ushered through the Stalinist terminal towards a Stalinist dining room, halting at a table set up at its entrance. In quirky syntax typical of the local twang, the seated couple asked us for foreign currency to pay for the banquet we were about to be served. Though highly irregular, I suggested to those around me simply to fork over the money and enjoy the adventure. We then filed into the hall, tables elaborately decorated—there was clearly a vegetable sculptor in residence—and took our seats. Platters immediately began appearing and the pace of the event seemed suddenly to accelerate. Though the ladles and chopsticks were flying about with much mirth abroad, the guests' curiosity only seemed to heighten as the banquet carried on. Hardly blaming them, I finally volunteered to make inquiry about the occasion.

No matter who I asked, I was told to speak to someone else, eventually finding myself shunted into the kitchen. There, at a very big table, clothless and completely unadorned, sat several people in uniforms, clearly from the plane, and the cook, whose state of disarray prevented me from considering him the chef. To one and all, or to no one, I asked, "Why are we here when we are so close to Beijing, our destination?" Peals of laughter came right back at me. I asked again, prefacing the question by raving about the food. After the second try, a chap jumped up, put his arm around me, and walked me around the table, stopping at the slovenly cook.

"Let me introduce you to this chef of great fame, an old friend of mine."

I went through the usual routine, expressing delight at meeting him, even suggesting that I might be aware of his reputation. I also cited some of the dishes for special mention, which pleased him no end; but when I asked again about the detour, the chef went silent and the CAAC crewmember took over again.

"How lucky we are! When we were about to leave Hong Kong, I heard that the chef would be working in Tianjin." I remained puzzled and it likely showed.

"It turns out that the chef was doing some special work at the airport and it was suggested that a banquet could be laid on for our 'foreign guests.' How could we turn down such an opportunity? We figured that a minor diversion from Beijing would surely be worth it. Now go and tell your friends how honored they should be that the chef was available to prepare such a feast." Feeling like an overly precocious schoolboy who had gotten up his teacher's nose, I was then turned around by the barking airman and sent on my way back to my table.

There they were, the lucky "foreign guests," staring at me, eager for an explanation. Without a hint of skepticism, I found myself enthusiastically passing on the message just delivered to me. These confused travelers who were likely shrewd and inquiring on their own turf were positively gleeful about the rip-off banquet, and I was right there with them though I suspected that some cadres had, in fact, canceled an event at the very last minute, leaving the chef and his fare high and dry.

As we walked back to the plane to reboard, the Englishman took my arm and breathlessly clucked about just how fabulous China is, commenting, "I'll never understand why you were so worried."

There was no point in even opening up *The Belton Estate*. Our flight to Beijing would be that short, and my companion, who had gone completely native, was already planning his return though he had not yet even arrived. Once we had, though, he insisted that I leave him to his own devices when the customs officer took exception to his paper work.

Calla Lilies

Patsy worked at the American Embassy in Beijing and was famous for having filled up several warehouses with antiques from her global postings. A tall and aristocratic woman, she was lucky to be thusly gifted in the apparent absence of a nervous system. There was talk of opening an antique shop in San Francisco; yet I always sensed that if her itinerant and compulsive buying were to stop, oblivion would await her. I would occasionally tag along on her sprees, watching the merchants light up as she neared them—mind you, the haunts were few in the Beijing of the early eighties.

My own favorite was the Theater Shop in Dongdan, a store packed with treasures and presided over by elderly gentlemen who had all owned substantial curio establishments prior to the coming of Mao Zedong. Off to the side of the main floor in a windowless niche of a room, there was a small rug emporium; and on my very last day in Beijing in 1985, when I went to say my farewells, the man in charge of that area nearly tackled me, gleeful that I had shown up because he had something right up my street. When I told him that my shipment had already gone, he would hear none of it, instantly producing the supplest of threadbare carpets, one sporting a golden dragon whose patina was enchanting. At its very top, there was a row of indecipherable characters, long blurred by much foot traffic. In a flash, it was folded into nothing and handed over to my friend, Claire, who had come with me. Luckily, her return to London from a Beijing posting at the British Embassy was not quite in the offing, and she kindly volunteered to send it on with her own things. That rug, by the way, turned out to have been made in Samarkand for the Palace and actually used in the Qing imperial library, identified as such by the dim calligraphy in the weave.

It was a treat to be invited to Patsy's house for supper. Since I lived in a hotel room with no kitchen, eating in a real home was a much-appreciated novelty. Although I did my level best to transform room 455 into an apartment, it just wasn't the same thing. Patsy's was an Aladdin's cave of treasures, every inch festooned with the spoils of her shopping excursions. There were textiles strewn across the furniture, ceramics obtained from under the counters at the Sunday bird market, and bird cages everywhere. For such a hostess, there was no way I was going to show up with some garish box of imported chocolates, the provenance of which could only have been too obvious: the lobby shop of my joint venture hotel.

Late in the afternoon on the day of the dinner party, I headed westward on Chang'an Boulevard to the Friendship Store, minding the broken sidewalks, toppling walls and rotting vegetables along the way. That the shop was four floors of often random kitsch, there was no doubt. Where else could one buy a snuff bottle with Friedrich Engels painted on the inside? I came to realize years later when living in London that Foyle's, the legendary bookstore, must have gotten its customer service model from this place: there was catatonic indifference amongst the staff towards the clientele and a payment system that taxed the customer. Several scraps of onion skin had to be filled out, chopped, brought to distant tills, then returned to the counter of purchase. Yet, the place was worth it, offering up genuine surprises from time to time.

As I wandered around the back of the ground floor, I came upon some flowers. Feeble attempts at some style always touched me regardless of the results. That a young woman, living in a world just emerging from the Cultural Revolution, could take pleasure—and want to impart that pleasure by attempting wispy and incongruous flower arrangements—warranted my warm attention; but empathy quickly turned to excitement. For behind her stood a vase of calla lilies! How she had gotten them was as mysterious as the sudden appearance of banana salesmen in the streets of Beijing, known for their canny black market currency transactions.

"I'll have them all," I said.

I then scurried around behind her make-shift counter and took the huge bunch in my hands, her terror only abating after I assured her that I was neither about to make a mad dash without paying nor concerned about an elaborate flower arrangement. All she had to do was bind the blooms so I could carry them. Though relieved by my non-threatening request, she also seemed somewhat disappointed by the fact that I did not value her artistic skills; but the prospect of a committee gathering to decide on how to cope with my calla lilies gave me the strength to opt for a bit of old newspaper. Sent on an excursion to pay for the blooms, my absence afforded her the time to get the job done. Then I was homeward bound.

As I retraced my steps back to the Jianguo Hotel, I felt like a character in a black and white movie, with only my flowers showing up in color. When I entered the lobby, the sight of the flowers caused pleasurable excitement to radiate from the bunch. Up in my room, I filled up the downstairs sink and placed the lilies in it to keep them fresh until the evening. Opposite that sink, by the way, was a tub that likely contained Beijing's complete stash of Tab, faithfully commandeered by my trusty driver. I then stretched out, put on some Handel and carried on with yet another Trollope novel. The television at the foot of my bed, of course, remained dark. Even on a Saturday night, the best program to be expected was a demonstration on how to use a leaf blower. I must have dozed off for awhile, pleased with the rare flowers soaking nearby.

Readied for the party and carrying Patsy's flowers, I returned to a lobby full of activity. Though the space itself was not that crowded, navigation was difficult. I soon realized that security concerns were thwarting my path. Recognizing my predicament, a room boy known to me rushed over and explained that the Premier himself was shortly coming to dine with the Prime Minister of Australia; thus, the delay which he reckoned would not be too long. There was no point in making a fuss so I decided simply to get as close to the entrance as I could to catch a glimpse of the dignitaries. With little effort, I found myself almost next to Bob Hawke, the very image of Oz incarnate. He suddenly turned towards the main doors of the hotel, obviously made aware that Zhao Ziyang was about to arrive. But before I could even focus on the approaching iconic reformer, some Australian flunky grabbed the flowers from my arms and transferred them into Bob Hawke's, who then presented them to his guest. In moments, I found myself standing virtually alone in the lobby, the circus having moved on and my path unobstructed.

I bought chocolates under duress and presented them to my hostess, along with a story about her calla lilies ending up in the arms of the Premier. No one believed me.

Tibet 1984

Access to a "back door"—the term used to describe indirect and effective networking in China—at the Chengdu branch of China Travel Service prompted me, weeks before, to make an inquiry about a trip to Tibet. But the subsequent silence led me to believe that the request had gone the way of so many others in China. Then, the "black banger," my antiquated telex machine, barked back: "permit available come immediate [sic]." Suddenly, my job mattered little and I was queuing up at the airport and bound for Sichuan, a province renowned for its hot peppers and the only viable transit point into Lhasa, the Tibetan capital, from China. Speaking of peppers, Deng Xiaoping hailed from Sichuan as well.

The man in front of me on the check-in line was burdened with watermelons. Although July was the height of their season in Beijing, they were hardly worthy of transport to the tropical southwest. But, Beijing is famous for watermelons in July so they would simply be expected at the other end. He could not resist commenting, "You really don't need a down coat in Chengdu at this time of the year." Although myself burdened with a kelly green jacket and sweat pouring from me, I feigned a casual tone saying that I was Lhasa-bound. His quizzical expression disappeared immediately, signaling that my anticipation of the cold Tibetan weather made as much sense as his watermelons.

Beijing is green in the summer only because every tree is watered by hand. I had forgotten what rain could do. The lushness of Chengdu enhanced the vacation spirit that had already settled over me upon leaving the capital. Mr. Hu, my "back door," was at the airport, his presence and attention heightening the welcome already provided by nature. Even the inevitable and hollow compliments about my Chinese—one need only grunt to be showered with praise—were pleasurable, but when we arrived at the hotel and it was time to pay, the hospitality of foliage and kind words quickly evaporated. When it came to foreign exchange, I was simply a cash cow. Yet as I peeled bills off into the hands of the surly clerk (Mr. Hu had receded into a corner of the comically monumental lobby as the transaction was occurring), I rationalized the indignity of the situation by chanting to myself, mantra-like, that, after all, I was actually on my way to Tibet. Considering how often I had been abused by taxi drivers who had grandly consented merely to take me from one foreign ghetto to another in Beijing, the prospect of making it to Tibet bridled my fury.

My three traveling companions were waiting for me at the airport early the next morning: Karin, a twenty-five year-old New Englander of Norwegian descent, teaching English at the local university and about to return to the States, and an overseas Chinese couple, Frank, an Ivy League professor, and his wife, Terry. After a flurry of introductions, Terry immediately let it be known that they were guests of a grateful government. Her husband had given a series of lectures on computer science at the invitation of the Chinese government in Beijing, and he was rewarded with a Tibet for-two excursion. After cross-examining me about just how much I was paying, she transformed the news of my fleecing into an exhortation of support for the motherland by urging Frank to reimburse their hosts for a trip they weren't paying for. (Aside from the infuriating fact that in the tiered pricing system overseas Chinese paid less than "foreign guests," payment for these sorts of trips was a purely internal matter, with the "people's currency," rather than foreign exchange, simply moving from one ledger to another. If Terry did manage to persuade Frank to write a check, such misplaced patriotism would be a bookkeeper's nightmare, or, more likely, graft in search of a home.) But we were still offering each other hard-boiled eggs in the airport waiting room so more small talk would just have to do. The same woman who had just spoken of debt to the motherland then went on, with resignation, to chronicle the gradual destruction of her own family in Nanjing, beginning with Liberation in 1949, then moving on to the Great Leap Forward during the fifties, and finally the decade of the Cultural Revolution, which started in 1966. It was the myth of the motherland, unsullied by her own exile or even the blood of her relatives, which drew her back to this place. I was on vacation, though, determined to escape temporarily the very Chinese labyrinth in which I lived and to which she had returned.

After hearing so much about Lhasa's twelve-thousand-foot altitude, I was focusing only on the prospect of passing out as soon as the plane's door swung open. But simply arriving in this sudden green valley, where the sky is so close that its color belongs on a cheap looking postcard, buoys the spirit. We teetered down steps mounted on a car resembling a hybrid vehicle that, years before, had been used by a big New York bank as a publicity stunt to popularize its willingness to make car loans. A university president and his family had been with us on the trip and were immediately engulfed by officials, leaving us on our own to gawk at a ring of mountains and that haunting sky. Suddenly, a four-wheel drive vehicle appeared right next to us. The driver got out, announcing first that he was to fetch the foreigners and then that the guide had been unable to come owing to some mix-up about our arrival. Evidently, we had been expected yesterday, and she simply was not up to making the trip two days in a row.

"How far is it to the guest house?" someone asked.

"About one hundred kilometers."

Although that sort of journey really did not seem so long, we all thought it wise to use the facilities before setting out anyway. We walked down the path whence the car had driven and came upon a terminal, very much a shrunken version of the Chengdu hotel, but it was locked. To the left, though, there was an out-house. After emerging, I could only pay attention again only once I had drawn air back into my lungs.

2

In Tibet, one must make a conscious effort not to keep looking up. Once the initial shock of the sky and mountains subsides, the pleasure of the human landscape takes over: broad faces dominated by quick eyes and teeth that looked capped, and a great sense of style. Both men and women sport colorful ribbons in artfully braided hair that is either piled high or allowed to tumble down the back. Turquoise dominates the extravagant jewelry that initially overpowers masterfully wrought silver and a variety of amulets. Their ready and disarming warmth came as a surprise. Considering the geographical isolation of the Tibetans and their bitter experience with the foreign Chinese, I had been quite prepared to deal with a local chill, but there was none.

Immediately out of the airport compound, there were no points of reference. The road disappeared and so did the people. The ride was hellish, but since I assumed that the rubble, at any moment, would give way to pavement, the leg room of the rear seat, which I had all to myself, outweighed the temporary discomfort caused by the broken road. Before traveling far, we found ourselves in a warren of walls washed white. Each of the doors to these medieval-feeling compounds was painted with a crescent and circle, and above it, a cornice holding a blue and white banner that rippled sensuously in the breeze. Atop each corner tower of the compound was placed a single uprooted tree, with branches accented by colorful flags. Since we were moving so slowly, I could tell that these flags were covered with script and a variety of busy designs. Some were in tatters. Once hung, they were evidently left forever to the elements. There did not seem to be flag maintenance—only additions to the display. Then, abruptly, as if squeezed through the village, we were again a part of this fearsome place. In the sudden absence of flags and folks that had just been bearing down on our vehicle, I gradually began to notice ruins that looked natural rather than man-made—their color in no way differed from the land around them. High above us, their size and complexity suggested once mighty structures. Owing to their lofty position, they still commanded the valley beneath them. With a squint, I could also see people and their grazing animals, and before we even had a chance to wave at the distant shepherds, they were waving at us.

Well into the journey now—time but not distance wise—I graciously volunteered my spacious back seat. The paved road had never come. This began a routine of rotation that took on greater importance as the reality of travel in Tibet took hold. For about an hour, following the bank of the broad and fast Brahmaputra River, we were pressed between cliffs and water. All along the way, workers seemed to be randomly chipping away at boulders in an apparent effort to broaden our path. But rocks seemed to be finding their way into considerable arrangements that inevitably blocked our way. As usual, the laborers beat us to the punch by greeting us as we crept amongst them. The warmth of summer had led many to discard their native garb for trousers and undershirts. From time to time, a few would stare blankly at us, much like cows can do as they stand in a pasture apparently oblivious to people passing before them. It suddenly dawned on me that they, in fact, were Chinese and not Tibetan. That look, which the foreigner had to suffer across the border, now seemed positively alien in the villages of Tibet.

At the end of the second hour, we came to a bridge that crossed the river. There were two graceless guardhouses flanking the approach beyond which soldiers were marching in lax formation on the bridge itself. Their maneuvers, coupled with a road crew's lame efforts at repairing a damaged railing, prevented us from taking full advantage of the paved way. Although we could not speed up, the simple pleasure of cement beneath our wheels compensated for further delay. Once again, I was sure that a roadway now lay before us. But the bridge was not a link to modern times. Rather, we began a journey along the Kyichu River that was simply a miserable continuation of the first. Soon again, we were passing in and out of villages. Despite their isolation from one another, cut off by various natural divides, their consistent "urban" style of architecture and clothing, as well as people's infectious good humor, indicated a continuum between the settlements that showed little respect for the very barriers separating them.

When a vehicle much like ours approached, its horn blowing, our driver smiled in recognition. With the cars finally side by side, we discovered that the other had been dispatched to fetch our bags. But, seasoned travelers that we were, we had only brought along carry-on luggage. Not annoyed by their futile trip, the baggage brigade instead roared with laughter; "We'll be paid no matter what." Immediately after passing us, the second car thrashed about in the rubble until it, too, was poised for home. For the next few hours, we had a bouncing shadow on our tail. While all this was going on, I happened to remember the old algebra problem about how long it would take for two trains to overtake each other. The question was moot in Tibet for two reasons: there were no trains and all moving vehicles appeared to be going at the very same speed.

Our driver grew more casual after the encounter with his colleagues, suddenly volunteering that he had been sent to Tibet from Sichuan well over a decade before, but he was vague about the circumstances of that relocation. It only took a bit of subtraction to figure it out: he was a stranded Red Guard. Sporting jaunty sunglasses and those curious high-heeled sandals currently the rage among Beijing boulevardiers, he was hardly the image of a crazed thug loosed on Tibet by the anarchy of the Cultural Revolution. Currently in the employ of China Travel Service, he was respectably shuttling the likes of us in and out of Lhasa.

Right after the road took a sharp turn to the left, the driver parked in the crook of the winding riverbank. The stop was well timed. After fanning out to respond to nature's call, we were all drawn back to a promontory. With the sky and mountains bearing down and the river's current perplexed by the sudden inlet, my mind immediately freed itself from political observation to make room for the splendor around me, and then the driver called to us. Turning on cue, we found ourselves beneath the gaze of a massive and garishly painted stone Buddha that looked beyond us, out over the very scene that had captured our attention. I felt disoriented, with nature and the figure's appreciation of it competing for my attention.

As we continued along our rocky way, more road crews presided over rubble that had just been chiseled from huge boulders. For sure, it was rubble now, but from within the heaps there gradually emerged hints of religious imagery and script that had been torn from the cliffs above. The blasting that echoed from distant valleys seemed less sinister than the rhythmic clatter of chisels heard right outside our car. The random violence of the Red Guards had been transformed into public works. The Tibetans, subjugated by the Chinese, were now doing the work begun by our congenial driver a decade before. Something caught the light. It was so distant that the glow seemed to come from beyond the horizon. Mirage-like, a golden roof emerged. It was the Potala, the red and white palace of Tibet's theocratic rulers, the Dalai Lamas, dating from the seventeenth century. Named for a holy Hindu mountain in southern India that was later shared by the Buddhists and dedicated to Avalokiteshvara, the Bodhisattva of Compassion, it now stands vacant, abandoned by its fourteenth occupant who fled to exile in India during 1959. Though initially a distraction from the discomfort of the ride, the Potala seemed to stay beyond our grasp—like a vanishing point on the landscape that toyed with our attention. The end of the ordeal was now linked to a landmark that did not draw near.

We soon reached another bridge, more of an overpass that again held the promise of pavement. Spanning a dry gully, it sported grillwork that was being painted bright blue and yellow by a crew of mature women. The rubble, however, continued right across the bridge. On the other side, we were quickly shunted off our path into a queue of trucks about to ford a fast-moving stream that did not even pass under the bridge. A convoy coming towards us, barring the right of way, held things up. For some reason, one of its trucks simply stopped on our side of the water; its driver got out and disappeared into a tented camp nearby. Since the abandoned truck now sat squarely at the very center of the only flat surface over which traffic could pass, those behind it risked being overturned as they crept along, leaning at a forty-five degree angle, between us and the obstacle. Despite the danger, we began taking perverse pleasure at seeing just how close each truck came to tipping over—right onto us. It was not until an open truck lumbered towards us, with a cargo known first to our noses, that the little game suddenly lost its charm. We barely got the windows up in time to avoid being splattered by the night soil coming right at us from the lurching lorry.

Suddenly, we were on a road, but just as quickly, we veered off of it to avoid hitting a wooden arm jutting out from an abandoned inspection station that was blocking the way. This well-worn detour had obviously been in place for quite some time. With the Potala now rushing towards us, the pace of life seemed to quicken. Rube Goldberg-like vehicles crisscrossed the road as Tibetans wove in and out of traffic on their appointed rounds. Looming pea green army-issue trucks were stuffed with Chinese soldiers in various states of undress, and dump trucks were piled high with stores and sleeping Chinese in cerise tank tops, a deliberately grotesque color used to thwart theft, we were told. So out of scale, these vehicles dwarfed the local hub-bub that went on beneath them, close to the ground. The shoulders running alongside the roadway turned green and small groups of naked children splashed in tiny pools that had likely been filled by recent rains. As a gentle ease settled over me, I spotted a rotting ox carcass just feet from the giggling bathers. Our turn to the left was so abrupt that the dead animal could have been taken for a driver's landmark. But the discomfort of this new route was offset by the soothing tunnel of willows through which we were passing. Then, at a gate that seemed more a trellis for the abundant white oleander surrounding it than an obstacle to our progress, an ornery adolescent in an army uniform hopped out of a guardhouse and officiously waved us to a halt with a limp red banner. It was hard to tell if he was new on the job or if the flag procedure had just been introduced. Whichever way, this clumsy brush with authority beneath propaganda billboards sporting the calligraphy of Mao Zedong was disorienting. In China proper these days, such messages are scarce. After all, its leader, Deng Xiaoping, is more than an economic pragmatist. He is also a survivor of the Great Helmsman's purges and the father of a son tossed out a window by Maoist supporters. We were permitted to pass with a grudging flick of the soldier's wrist. But, there were more gates to get through, and on each were placards identifying subsequent compounds as dormitories for various work units; but the presence everywhere of milling soldiers said otherwise. Our lodgings at guest house number three were clearly in the middle of a military garrison.

3

A Miss Peng came out on to the concrete porch, greeting us in a shrill falsetto suited for Peking opera. An enormous white sun hat protected her prized complexion, all the whiter in this land of high color. Since lunch was being held for us she suggested that we simply unload the car and worry about settling in later. We dutifully obeyed, and the service staff stood by as spectators, watching as we clumsily regained our land legs after the five-hour ordeal. As if to warn us, a huge oxygen tank stood just inside the door. Karin tossed her bags down and bounded out ahead of us, up the graded path to the dining room. Abruptly, her shoulders and then her head drooped, and she passed out. Miss Peng had obviously been through this before. As we raced towards our fallen comrade, ignoring the very lesson just observed, Miss Peng routinely filled an enormous canvas bag with oxygen from the tank and forced its long hose into slumped Karin's mouth. Coming to, she mumbled something about respect for nature.

The dining room, yet another version of a cavernous lobby, could have been a foreigner's pen anywhere in China—except the Tibetan waitress and I were both foreigners communicating in a third language, Chinese. A group of geriatric Germans eating the simple Chinese fare with great gusto shamed us into lame good cheer that masked neither our exhaustion nor Karin's pallor. But the simple pleasure of being at rest stifled any urge we might have had to make clever remarks about the surroundings.

Just as the ox carcass along the road had changed the mood, so did Miss Peng's sudden reappearance. She stalked towards us, clearly on a mission. With her was Miss Wang, introduced as a manager of the compound as well as a travel official. Promptly, Miss Wang started waving onion-skin receipts in our faces. There had been a mistake in Chengdu's calculations. If we wanted to go on to Shigatse, the capital of Tsang province, a substantial supplement would have to be paid. All I could remember was parting with all those fifties back in the Chengdu hotel lobby. Although Karin and I, the two long-term foreign residents in China, objected as one, we knew full well that all had already been lost. Terry, of course, the disenfranchised guest of the state, took the high road. "Mistakes do happen. Everything has to be expensive here. Even petrol has to be imported." We paid and she did not.

Karin's collapse earlier and the onset of an excruciating headache readily persuaded me to heed Miss Wang's advice about taking it easy for the rest of the day. I can only compare sleep that night to the delirium of fever—without the heat, and the next morning, much as the elderly do, I swore that I had slept not a wink. Not far behind the Kitaro-like music that had awakened me came the rhythm of a hammer hitting rock, punctuated by blasting. Kitaro, in fact, turned out to be the reverberation of Chinese propaganda being barked over microphones within this amphitheater of mountains. Awkward bathroom arrangements—we had to pass through Terry and Frank's suite only to find the door forever locked—and the endless wait for an unwanted breakfast sadistically delayed our departure from the compound. Lhasa remained beyond the gates.

When we finally did leave, our first stop was a park offering a good view of the Potala. I felt as though I was on the very border between China and Tibet. The park really could have been back in Beijing, with its pounded earth and painted railings long marbled by rust that enclosed ersatz Suzhou rock formations. I stared up at the very symbol of Tibet, its color that of a villa in Chianti—the red of iron-rich fields—haphazardly festooned in a rainbow of ragged pennants. After a good look, I walked back to the car past blue-suited Chinese strolling around the park and two Tibetan fellows, leaning up against one of those railings, playing local instruments. Merriment at their own music along with the casual and high style of their clothing— putting only one arm into one sleeve seems to be the vogue— reminded me that I was on holiday.

Back in the car and bound for our next stop, we asked to be dropped at a distance from the Jokhang, the most sacred temple in Tibet, dating from the seventh century. Even before Miss Wang could begin saying "no," we sensed that we were already near and flung open the car doors and were on our way. A decrepit compound of houses was between the traditional Tibetan hospital where we now stood and the Temple off in the distance. We quickly entered a maze of muddy lanes that took us vaguely in the direction of the Jokhang. The squalor of the area was indisputable, but the whitewashed houses and their cloth cornices—predominantly white with a stripe of blue that seemed deliberately to catch the breeze in seductive waves—were distractions from the filth. Well along the way, we suddenly came upon rubble and bulldozers. The neighborhood was evidently being razed from the center outwards, but people still were holding to byways invisible to us in the absence of buildings on either side. We were now in a no-man's land of motorcycles with sidecars and Chinese Keystone cops. Even back in Beijing, there is something comical about authority. The hats are never really on straight, the uniforms do not seem to fit quite right and the inevitable crowd of totally deadpan onlookers just do not seem to mesh with tales of the Cultural Revolution and the occupation of Tibet. But here in Lhasa, people shunned the Han Chinese now occupying their ghost town and moved as one toward the moat of faithful circling the Jokhang.

I had seen aerial photographs of a grander version of this scene—the Muslims at Mecca. Though I have never been on the Hajj, I can only guess at the tone of the experience. This crowd, apparently lacking such obvious intensity, seemed at ease with the gravity of their clockwise circumnavigation, but no less reverent. As we drew close to the Temple's forecourt, that all changed. Pilgrims who had evidently traveled hundreds of miles were now going through identical, though not synchronized, obeisance. In the manner of an exercise class, each first stood, then squatted, then finally lay prostrate. The entire ritual was punctuated by random claps and the sound of sandpaper rubbing along the stones. Most had rough coverings strapped to their palms for protection against their apparently endless display of devotion.

4

Since admission to the Jokhang could only be gained through the good offices of Miss Wang, we were actually pleased to see her awaiting us. Then, snaking our way through the agile pilgrims towards the darkness into an inner entrance, she went ahead to sort out the tickets. She finally emerged to tell us that a delegation of high-ranking Chinese cadres from Hangzhou was now being shown around, and we would have to come back in about an hour. After agreeing to meet up again, we bolted and were quickly caught up in the ambling crowd whose casual spirit was periodically disrupted by the occasional Chinese, oblivious to the clockwise flow around them. Various people sidled up to us, offering jewelry, largely of luminous turquoise and coral, as well as bone. Delicately carved religious figures housed in hammered silver were the most appealing. But tales of rigorous customs inspection upon departure from Lhasa airport prevented any serious consideration of such icons. Souvenirs even hinting of religion were said to be summarily seized by the authorities. Old cowbells and a bridle piece that hung from a tented stall seemed a safe bet, though. With the help of bilingual Tibetans and good cheer engendered by incredulity over my interest in such objects, I was able to negotiate the purchase and even obtain my first Sanskrit receipt. (Despite my loathing for those endless bits of tissue paper, the unpleasantness caused by not having one upon the demand of some Chinese clerk was to be avoided.) The difficulty of imparting the notion of a receipt, however, was compounded by the question of currency. Within China, there are two scripts: one used by locals and the other, by foreigners. Although officially there is parity between the two, *waihui*, denied to the Chinese, was required to buy foreign goods. Thus, if the Chinese wanted to buy imported items, they were unable to do so with their own currency, *renminbi*.

Back in Beijing, a brisk black market was developing. Students and "foreign experts" present in China through cooperative official arrangements carried a card that permitted use of *renminbi* where *waihui* was required. With an unofficial exchange rate of two to one or even three, foreigners allowed to use the "people's currency" were doing rather well, and the Chinese were finding most creative arrangements that would allow them to purchase symbols of status. It was less the nature of the goods than the fact that they had been purchased by a clever subversion of currency restrictions that put swagger in the step of a chauffeur emerging from the Friendship Store carrying a cuckoo clock.

I mention all this because the Tibetans did not want the cherished *waihui* offered for the bells and bridle. They had obviously never seen these crisp bills bearing English words, so unlike the flaccid and dirty specie of the Chinese realm. Although I tried to explain its value, payment simply had to be in *renminbi*. Without warning, a man appeared next to me, offering to do an exchange. Since I was over a barrel and he knew it, it was parity or no deal. Thus, he got his *waihui*, I got the bells and bridle, and the stall owner got a wad of *renminbi*. The bells turned out to be a real crowd pleaser. Draped across my arm, they attracted a variety of people who were anxious to give the leather band on which the bells were mounted a good tug. It was a noisy procession that now saw us back to the entrance of the temple.

Within striking distance of the forecourt, I abruptly took the bells off my arm and shoved them in my shoulder bag. Considering the lack of public reverence surrounding us in the shadow of the Jokhang, my misplaced gesture of respect held meaning only for me, and put a damper on the goings on. Once again, we walked among and over the people making their obeisance. Despite the intensity of their busy prayers—each believer kept track of his efforts on beads while getting up and down—they managed to include us in their sights, openly and warmly.

With the officials from Hangzhou now gone, we were free to enter the complex. Huge golden prayer wheels were on our left, the spinning of which transmitted embossed messages on pilgrims' behalf heavenward. The notion of repetition and the circle were clearly powerful components of Tibetan religious life. At the very moment I was trying to be profound about these observations, monks, standing on a balcony above us, waved and shouted their greetings. We were then led by others through a pitch-black passage into an open courtyard whose walls were lined with racks of prayer wheels the size of big coffee cans. Walking clockwise of course, I found myself giving the wheels a good spin, all the while coping with an assault of color— the temple's exterior, at the courtyard's center, was rusty red and orange, the overhanging roof animals, gold, and that sky, a blue scrim setting off all beneath it.

The inside of the temple was a virtual bazaar of imagery, with a soaring ceiling that emphasized close proximity to layers of statuary, relics, paintings, and textiles. The smell of burning yak butter just heightened the atmospherics. Rather than affording a pilgrim room for perspective and contemplation, this microcosm squarely put him in his place, impaling him on a riot of symbols. The sky is all but forgotten in a place like this. Climbing up to the roof, we suddenly found ourselves in the very middle of a menagerie of those gilded animals. From yet another vantage point, the Potala again asserted itself over the valley and over me. As I wandered around the roof looking over the old city, I suddenly heard waves of chants from no apparent source. Atop some distant roof, I noticed files of women walking in cadence—back and forth—pounding staffs as they sang. But owing to the distant sound's delay in reaching me, the singing and pounding seemed somehow disconnected from the women's performance. Their task was not readily apparent until I remembered seeing some footage back in Beijing taken by a network cameraman. This very scene—the tamping of earth to construct a new roof— was now before me, but this moment of association was dashed by a monk's fumbling with my bag. As if my own rapture were somehow at odds with the experience, a holy man whom one would have expected to share this wonderment opened my bag, grabbed those bells that I had bought in the market, and began scampering around the roof, shaking them wildly. I was always being reminded that experiences could not be compartmentalized neatly into frames—awe and silliness were just fine at the very same time.

5

After lunch back at the stockade that no one really wanted, we went to Norbulinka, the summer home of the Dalai Lama, built in the fifties. Upon admission, we were of course told that each interior photograph would cost twenty *renminbi*. A boxy old radio atop a velvet cushion appeared to be an object of worship, and furniture that really belonged in a doctor's office and a collage of people through the ages paying obeisance to a Dalai Lama of the past were more amusing than camera-worthy; but when it came to the pristine "toilet" and its fine carpet, I could not resist—and there was no charge. Frankly, it was a relief to pass quickly through this place into the courtyards, with their striped walls of red, orange, and green afire in the sun and set off by the stark white of adjoining buildings. The foolish interiors were somehow vaporized, turning these open spaces beneath the sky into the chambers of a real palace.

At my request, we went to the Bank of China. It was in a compound, simply one door in a long one-story building housing many work units, identified as the LASA (sic) Branch. I walked in and introduced myself to the first clerk, handing him my bilingual card and telling him that Manufacturers Hanover was one of America's largest banks. I then proceeded to the next row of desks. As my eyes focused in the dark room, I spotted the branch manager, a real "Dragon," ensconced against the back wall. Once again, I introduced myself and passed out a card to her second line of defense. By then, my first card was being passed back to her, hand over hand, and a shout, "one of America's largest banks," rang out just as my credentials reached her desk, the vortex of power. She slowly emerged into the light, holding my card in one hand and flicking it with two fingers of the other, all the while sizing me up. With a big smile, I greeted her warmly in that crackling Chinese so typical of Beijing. I managed to drop as many names of senior officials from Bank of China's head office as possible, transforming them from those I might see at some dreary banquet into workaday colleagues who had sent their best regards. Relieved at not having to deal with a foreign language and mindful of my apparent intimacy with her distant bosses, she welcomed me. Since I had no desire to burden our conversation with the formality of an official call, I quickly shifted gears, telling her of my wanderings around China, citing spots that inevitably evoke automatic associations: Hangzhou and beautiful women, Kunming and eternal spring, Shanghai and hairy crabs. With tea came small talk. During the Cultural Revolution, she had found her way to Tibet and subsequently married a Chinese in Lhasa. The zealotry that had likely brought them here and their part in the madness that spilled out of Maoist China into Tibet seemed somehow irrelevant to this exchange with a minor bureaucrat stranded a long way from home. "You are the first American banker ever to visit us here," she said, escorting me out onto the marigold-lined path.

On our way to the Sera Monastery which, until the Chinese occupation, served as a center of monastic erudition and drew believers from all over Tibet into a cosmopolitan community of education, we again passed beneath the Potala, with the sky and mountains heightening its intensity. Looking off to the right, I noticed the Sera's bleached white buildings cascading off the range into the valley. Above this phosphorescent blur emerged towers that same color of iron-rich soil, topped by golden animals and giant amulets. As we got closer, the now familiar banners, dead trees at corners atop parapets strung heavily with colored swatches, frisky puppies, and busy people all quickened the monolith into a human enclave. We got out of the jeep and walked on sand toward the chanting halls on an avenue running between lamas' quarters. The weathered blue and red doors into these dormitories, with ornate and tarnished hardware and cloth flowing from their lintels, transformed our way into a gallery lined with Joseph Cornell-like boxes hanging in every portal. At the end of this avenue, we climbed atop a platform that led to a main hall but found ourselves quickly outside again. It turned out that we were on a roof, standing behind the very golden animals that had loomed in the distance during our approach to the monastery. After finally turning away from them, I found myself facing rugged, sloping hills and boulders painted with fanciful animals. A menagerie now sandwiched me in on the roof of the Sera. Down below again, the floor of the main hall was covered with lanes of carpet, piled at regular intervals with religious looking garb, each topped with a distinctive yellow hat to be worn by a monk. Banners were everywhere, and even the space left between the streaming textiles seemed to be filled with the heady smoke of the yak butter that burned throughout the hall. Side chambers were opened to us, some doors covered by thick chain mail. Once again, we entered the frantic environs of the gods. While our Chinese guide, Miss Peng, readily ticked off a "Who's Who" of Tibetan deities, her antiseptic delivery reflected an attitude of antiseptic disinterest. In one of these rooms, at the foot of a fierce statue, was a hole. I was urged to bow and put my head through it for good luck. Though scared, I did it. As it turns out, the hole was loosely covered by a leather sleeve on the other side so my head ended up in a bag—hardly in the universe of delightful frights that I had expected. Despite inquiries, I never did find out what that exercise was all about.

On to the next hall with its demons, banners, burning yak butter, and mothers with their babies. There were also walls lined with sutras, the holy books of the Buddhists. I asked to see one and the attending lama gladly agreed. Its leaves were printed horizontally, with each volume covered in wood and saffron colored cloth. The room was also crowded with reliquaries, holding the ashes of abbots and lamas, with bases of bronze or silver covered in huge semi-precious stones, all glistening in the candlelight. Amidst this religious clutter, I began strolling with Frank, the overseas Chinese professor. His wife's remarks about her devotion to the motherland still troubled me and we chatted about the masochism of her viewpoint. It dawned on me that his wife was no less a victim than the Tibetans; at least they were not being done in by their own. Already late in the day, we walked back to the car in silence. Tomorrow we would visit the Potala.

6

The morning was glorious as the jeep struggled up the rugged incline to the Potala, with the driver executing some pretty treacherous maneuvers to get us where we wanted to go. An unexpected passenger had joined us—a soldier from Terry's hometown. As soon as we stopped, I hopped out, eager to put distance between myself and the uniformed Chinese. After all, he was a member of the army of occupation. I spotted an elderly European couple whom I recognized from our compound and made straight for them. We passed gradually into the Potala, its red color growing black as the light lost its way through a baffle of corridors. Save the torches of guiding lamas, we proceeded in darkness. At one point, a monk standing behind me moved—I thought he had been a statue!—and the old girl whose arm I was supporting suddenly and out of necessity became my support. By far, the most impressive of the myriad halls was the one housing the remains of the fifth Dalai Lama. Supposedly, he is embalmed in a kneeling position within a five ton golden reliquary. It really is not the gold that is noteworthy but rather the intimidation of being forced up against so massive a monument with nowhere to turn.

After passing through a series of pantheons varying in their intensity, we found ourselves in a pavilion atop a roof set aside for tea, where we enjoyed a much-needed rest spent largely in silence. We then scattered, as if by tacit agreement. I sidled along a walkway that took me higher along a building that led to the Potala's white section. Shortly after sitting down on some chiseled stones that might someday find their way into a restored section of the compound, I was joined by three Tibetan boys saying "Dalai Lama" and pretending to take pictures. I offered to take a photo of one of them, but that was not what they wanted. I offered them the camera to take one of me—wrong again. I then tried out some Chinese, to which one boy responded. What they wanted were photos of the Dalai Lama. Evidently, foreigners bring them into Tibet and hand them out as souvenirs. Having come from within China, I frankly had neither thought of this nor could have done anything about it even if I had. I asked them where they lived. "East of the Potala, with all the other Tibetans," I was told. It was clear that we were facing west, with its new, institutional blocks laid out beneath our gaze. They worked on the Potala, earning about a dollar a day—an amount that did not apparently displease them. Just then, Frank, whom I introduced as an American, appeared. "Is America further away than India?" they asked—I suspect that any country to which the Dalai Lama had fled would have defined the horizon of their universe. Suddenly, the jeep appeared. As we pulled away, I waved until I could see them no longer.

That afternoon, we were handled: a traditional Tibetan hospital with simultaneous tours being conducted in Spanish, German and English, a carpet factory whose boss was not available for a chat because of diarrhea, and a traditional dance performance where I made a fool of myself trying to photograph the most beautiful girl I had ever seen. The sun retreated and it was back to the guest house for dinner and a propaganda film starring the Panchet Lama, the spiritual leader second only in stature to the Dalai Lama, but who is loved within China proper. Possibly a victim of his own survival, he now spends most of his time passing out ceremonial white scarves the way Elvis used to at his concerts.

The next morning Frank was suddenly forced to leave owing to his wife's discomfort in this altitude. I gave him some peanut butter and bread for their early morning journey back to the airport. As we said our fond good-byes—he stood in my room decked out in red pajamas—he blurted out that he felt like Alec Guinness in *The Bridge Over the River Kwai*. His last words were those of regret. "What's happening in Tibet is reminiscent of the Incas, or the Mayan civilization," he reflected.

7

The greatest issue facing me that dawn was whether or not to take my down coat to Shigatse. Remembering the watermelons and stifling heat in Beijing, I could not bear to think that I had carried it all this way for nothing. I grabbed it and strode out the door. When the car pulled up, there was a new driver and an extra passenger. Since Frank and his wife had left and our old driver had taken them to the airport, Mr. Zeng, our new chauffeur, was no surprise, but Miss Zhu, planted right in the front seat, was.

Our route was taking us to the bridge crossing back to the Brahmaputra River. Right before the large painted Buddha, about an hour out of Lhasa, I had to urinate. We stopped and I discovered a narrow slit of an entrance to a cave. My pleasure at the convenience and privacy was short lived; there were rats crawling all over feces. Since the call of nature was urgent, I began stamping my feet, but, as soon as I stopped, they reappeared. Trying to do two things at once only caused me to do yet a third. My laughter echoed through the rocks.

As we pushed on to the river over the tortuous course, we began saying "Where's the bridge?" in a way that a commercial had tried to discredit a competing hamburger chain with an old woman barking, "Where's the beef?" Miss Peng picked up on this and aped our husky rendition in her shrill tones. Finally, we reached the bridge, hoping that the southern route to Shigatse would be less arduous. Immediately upon crossing the river, we turned right, away from the airport road, much to our relief. As we comfortably drove on, it became obvious that there had been blasting along the way since the shoulders were littered with fragments of sculpture and carved Sanskrit. It dawned on me that our smooth ride was actually over pulverized relics of the past. We shortly began to climb into the mountains, passing goats barely perched on inclines in apparent defiance of gravity. The road grew more frightening, especially after a truck barreled around a corner and almost drove us off the cliff. Although the growing cold added an unwelcome edge to the ascent, I was a bit smug about donning my green down jacket that, all agreed, had finally come in handy.

Enveloped by mist at the summit, we stared at a shrine of trees heavy with banners, each a different color and covered with religious messages. Surrounding the shrine were piles of stones, deliberately arranged in a manner suggesting David Smith's sculptures. Looking over to the other side of the mountain, we were startled to see the huge Yardog Lake beneath us, more the color of the Caribbean than a body of fresh water in Tibet. The glorious hue that had so distinguished the skies now seemed to come up toward us through the clouds from below. We then descended, gradually reaching the road along the banks of the lake, passing through occasional settlements with their walls of beige, unfired brick, and corners bedecked with uprooted trees flying those now familiar banners. The doors sported that ubiquitous design of a circle above a crescent. Along this road, we stopped for lunch, taking our meager fare right to the water's edge. We were cold and exhausted by the journey and light-headed from the rapid descent from the nineteen-thousand-foot summit. All I could keep down was a piece of bread with some strawberry jam, which tasted extraordinarily delicious. Spam also appeared, the mere thought of which nauseated me. Our Chinese companions evidently were not similarly afflicted as they devoured everything in sight, inventing a new delicacy that evoked Dr. Seuss: spam spread with jam.

Three Tibetan girls seemed to appear from nowhere to witness our picnic. A hailstorm seemed to have followed the girls and was soon upon us. We bolted to the car as quickly as the thin air would permit, and continued around the lake where the landscape abruptly changed. Glaciers and safflower fields could be seen in the same glance. I suddenly noticed earthen totems along the road and began holding forth on the anthropological implications of their presence in this part of the world. They turned out to be electrical poles.

8

About eight hours into the trip, what seemed to be a mini-Potala appeared on the horizon. It was the mighty fort of Gyantse, testimony to the town's fifteenth century status as the capital of a kingdom located at the junction of various trade routes. Gyantse had also been the center of the Tibetan wool trade with India. Passing through a maze of alleys, we proceeded on to the Kumbum Monastery, built at the same time as the fort and renowned for its shape—ascending symmetrical stories and a golden cap. As we drove, I could not get over the Tibetans' reactions to our presence. They are backward and isolated, to be sure, yet they responded to us in ways that were delightfully predictable, completing a circuit of recognition virtually inconceivable between the Chinese and foreign strangers.

Just inside the courtyard, our driver ran over the leg of a snoozing dog. The yelp was piercing, but the driver's casual "*Mei shi*" ("It's nothing") transformed my discomfort into disgust for my Chinese companions as we made so barbarous an entrance. We then heard singing and pounding. Looking up, we saw women and children on one of the temple's terraced levels tamping down new earthen works as they chanted together. They beckoned us to come up. A monk gladly admitted us and gestured that we move clockwise within the holy place. Peeking into every doorway looking for a staircase, we kept coming upon rooms crowded with statues and covered with murals. Finally, at the last possible entrance before reaching the portal where we had been greeted by the monk—somehow calmed by ritual rather than delayed by inconvenience—we were able to ascend. Feeling pretty frisky, I bounded up the stairs but was quickly reminded of the altitude. I grasped at the wall for support and waited for the light-headedness to pass. Outside on the balcony, we were in the midst of rhythmic music sung by beautiful women and ragamuffins with running noses. There was much restoration going on with people pounding the earth and singing, the prayer wheels spinning and the lamas praying.

Considering that the ultimate goal of Buddhism is escape from rebirth, the texture of life certainly gave value to those who had not yet managed to do it. When we left the enclave, we warned the driver to look out for dogs. Back on the road, I once again marveled that despite the great distances traveled—more a matter of geography than miles—there was continuity in architecture, dress, and attitude. This is no mean task considering the obstacles separating these pockets of population. It is the religious denominator that has so readily transcended mere mountains and miles.

The mountains appeared striped with rust and green, probably evidencing mineral deposits, but when patterns of light passing through strange cloud formations hit the slopes, it was difficult to concentrate on natural resources beyond the beauty. Further on, I noticed that the trees lining the road appeared to be in adobe planters. Actually, they were surrounded by bricks after already having been planted, a practice similar to the surrounding of trees in the middle of a large field with walls, something I had seen often in our travels around China. After passing through several Chinese encampments, we finally arrived in Shigatse, the seat of the Panchen Lama. It appeared that in proportion to the native population, the percentage of foreign soldiers was higher here than in Lhasa. This was hardly a city, with only a few low-slung buildings. The local government headquarters, made of pink stucco more in keeping with Miami Beach than Tibet, dominated the scene. As in Lhasa, we were driven into an encampment behind high gates. There were rows of bunkers, all nondescript, except for the one which was fronted with six foot pink foxgloves—that one was ours.

Off each entry were two rooms with washstands and kettles of water in the common hall. The bathroom, clean to the eye, was in a separate building, and it had holes in the floor. But the intensity of the smell, noteworthy even for Tibet, was the best reason neither to eat nor drink. Since we were the only foreigners in residence, the dining room at the other end of the compound was empty save us. The marinated red and green peppers on the table reminded me of my aunt's fare back in New York. As a child, I loved watching her put them right on the gas burners before skinning and pickling them. All the vegetables looked fresh, but we were simply too tired to enjoy them. The real pleasure was simply being out of a moving vehicle. Despite exhaustion, we decided to stroll around the village. Right outside the gate, there was a display case with an exhibit of photos chronicling the life of Mao Zedong. Beyond the few immediate blocks surrounding the compound, life quickly grew relaxed. Mothers urged their toddlers toward us and folks were out for a *passeggiata*, many working skeins of raw wool onto spools as they chatted and strolled. The Chinese filtered out of their enclosures as well, in tight groups all dressed in white shirts over slacks in sharp contrast to the flare of the Tibetans. Despite the dirt, there was again great style here—not only in terms of dress, but in the way the Tibetans carried themselves. In the end though, even the mountains, clouds, sky, and fashion could not prevent us from fading, and we headed back to the guest house.

Bread with no salt, just like in Florence, seemed to be a breakfast specialty. I could not help but think fondly of the strawberry jam that we had eaten along the shore of the lake on our way to Shigatse. But maybe the combination of little appetite and a meager morning meal was a blessing. Mr. Hao, the manger of the compound, appeared and announced that he would be personally accompanying us to Taskilhunpo Monastery, the Panchen Lama's equivalent of the Potala. Mr. Hao had been here for seventeen years, his wife and daughter left behind in Chengdu. The matter-of-fact account of his loneliness was nonetheless touching, and it somewhat blunted the offense of his demeanor: nicotine stains seeping out from the spaces between his teeth, a fawning manner, and a total unwillingness to say anything of substance about Tibet. Yet over the years, he had managed to teach himself English, an Indian dialect, and Tibetan.

At the monastery, we were met by a lama who took us first through a warren of alleys—the buildings were largely monks' quarters—to a hall of chanting clerics. They sat side by side in rows, swathed in mustard colored robes, and most held staffs straight up in the air with large drums attached to the tops. They beat them with sticks shaped like scythes, tipped with padding that would strike the drum. The leader, dressed in maroon robes, maintained cadence with cymbals—one held in his upturned palm and struck with the other. There were a few men blowing small horns from time to time, and another pair, deep in the shadow of a corner, made sounds through extremely long horns—like alphorns—that rested on the floor. There were flies everywhere and the smell of yak butter permeated the hall. These comforting chants and rhythms came from men with a sense of ensemble born of years of practice and shared beliefs. In the midst of this, Miss Zhu started chattering away, enquiring about which Panchen Lama had first lived here or whether the golden decorations were, in fact, plated or solid. I used to admire the irreverent atmosphere of a Taiwanese temple or a Cantonese opera house, so unlike the pious silence of their western counterparts. But when Miss Zhu could not even bother to feign interest or when Mr. Hao lit up a cigarette and was told to put it out—after seventeen years here—that very offhand indifference I had, at times, enjoyed was certainly not appreciated in my traveling companions at this moment.

9

We next found ourselves in a large central courtyard. A group of lamas were apparently presiding over a market within a recessed promenade running along one side of a building. Local people were standing within the courtyard a few feet beneath the clerical merchants, with small stacks of clothing the object of their common attention. From what I could gather, people evidently donated clothing that was then sold by the lamas back to them to raise funds for the monastery. The indirection of the process was somehow preferred to explicit charity. We bought a few of the woolen aprons that are an integral part of the usual Tibetan garb for women. Frankly, it was hard to tell if the material was laden with lanolin because it was new or saturated with yak butter because it was old, but either way, they were pretty ripe. The lamas were most attentive to us but life did not stop because we were foreigners. They tended to our business and then moved on to others.

In the printing shop lined with wood blocks further on, we were permitted to take photographs with no charge. Rather than the deity and lama-cramped chambers of worship, it was frankly this type of place that offered an opportunity to ponder a bit of Tibet in knowable terms. Here, monks at work were no less involved in lives of prayer than their brethren lost in chanting, sitting opposite each other while one held the block and inked it and the other applied the paper. Multicolored banners of cheese cloth bore scriptures and images destined for those omnipresent trees that function as shrines; they were also hanging to dry around the room. Sutras were piled up, page by page, and retired prayer wheels rested in a window seat, barely catching stray rays of light that managed to persevere through deep passages from the outside.

The kitchen's atmospherics could have been captured by Rembrandt: gigantic copper cauldrons were set into a raised platform, wood burning with a fire ablaze beneath, huge copper ladles, and various cooking implements arranged in hanging rows along the wall, all in the dim light filtered through the escaping smoke. We trotted in and out of more prayer rooms—more grotesque and kindly images, more shimmering silk umbrellas, more burning yak butter, more flies, more monks, more mounds of barley flour piled high by pilgrims. Everything present was present to excess; and by the time that our visit had come to an end, I relished escape into the fresh air. Within sight of the waiting car, the lama who was leading us suddenly veered to the left. I could not bear the thought of another clockwise walk around a dark prayer hall. Instead, we emerged in yet another courtyard alive with chatter and clapping. Monks were conducting philosophical debates, one in each group somehow recognized as a referee, emphasizing a participant's point by clapping his outstretched hands after a theatrical wind-up. There was such infectious pep among these contending men that, dispatched on our way by their enthusiasm, we chattered all the way home.

After returning to the compound, I found myself alone with Miss Peng and decided to bring up Miss Zhu's permanence in the front seat during the grueling journey to Shigatse, and beyond that, her very presence. Miss Peng, after all, was on the job and had a far greater right to a comfortable seat than her colleague who was literally just along for the ride. Miss Peng, only mildly defensive, said that the driver needed to be chatted up over the course of this endless trip—especially after lunches. "Why can't you do that?" I asked. She then assured me that she would occupy the rear seat all the way back to Lhasa so Miss Zhu could stay put next to the driver, thereby assuring our comfort in the middle row of the Toyota Land Cruiser. I told her that the object of my remarks was not her torture in the back of the bus. It was Miss Zhu who would have to switch and, after having already occupied the catbird seat all the way here, should not be eligible for that seat on the way back. She promised to take it up with Miss Zhu and the tuckered out driver.

That afternoon, there was one last monastery to see on the outskirts of Shigatse. After driving about a half hour whence we had come, we left the road, driving in the shadows of mountains with no clear path before us. I suddenly became aware of a sparse number of people going about some sort of business, hinting at a community. As we drove on, the numbers thickened, with some fields of barley under cultivation and mules hauling piles of unfired bricks. Then, the familiar banners appeared at corners of walls, indicating a settlement. Once again, as we passed these isolated folks living in another era, we were charmed by the ease of our welcome. The object of our journey, the Zhalu monastery, dates from the eleventh century and was being restored inchmeal. Evidently, it had suffered more damage during the Cultural Revolution than in the nine hundred years leading up to it.

Lamas were again returning here and workmen, in their fashion, seemed to be tackling an apparently impossible task. We had to cross over a rather deep and wide ditch being dug by a gang of young men, the object of their labors not apparent. Last in our queue, I was served well by my long legs. I was able to leap across, landing cleanly on the other side. In a round of applause and good-natured hoots, I bowed low from the waist, with a good laugh all around.

The monastery is known for its distinctive green roof tiles, an ironic testimony to ancient Chinese patronage, as well as its wall paintings. A lama attempted to show us the famous murals, but the chambers were pitch black, illuminated only by a hand held match or a distant window. At one point, my eyes, having adjusted to the surroundings, made out the innards of a hall. Flanked by piles of yak skins, its entrance led into a room strewn with leaves of sutras; this had once been the monastery's library, founded by the Zhalu's fourteenth century abbot, Bunton Rinchen Drup. A synthesizer of disparate texts, he compiled a series of volumes that survived until the Cultural Revolution, when they were destroyed by the Red Guards. A short while later, when passing a window that looked out onto gilt animals that were atop the entrance of all monasteries, the lama offered us small clay squares imprinted with religious images. Miss Peng and Miss Zhu chose the most colorful and we, the most austere. On our way out, we again had to deal with the ditch, and since my leap was remembered, I was again expected to perform. The pressure was on and I regretted my earlier successful performance, but I made it.

10

At supper that night after Miss Zhu and the driver had left the dining room, Miss Peng told us of a solution she had worked out to the seating problem in the van: she and Miss Zhu would sit in the front and the two of us in the second row. I decided to remain silent, letting Karin react to a plan that avoided my earlier objections and had evidently met with opposition from the principals. My traveling companion was emphatic in her objection to Miss Zhu's continued presence in the front seat, eloquently stating that if Chinese were to come to America, we would insist upon their taking seats of honor; furthermore, we were paying! After all objections had been voiced, Miss Peng nonetheless asked what we thought of her plan. We expressed our displeasure clearly. There was obviously more to this situation than we could know, yet any further willingness to be culturally sensitive simply disappeared with the thought of the trip back to Lhasa under circumstances similar to those under which we had arrived. We sent Miss Peng back into the belly of the beast for another round. With the prospect of the return nightmare staring us in the face, we reacted in a similar fashion—unbridled giddiness. Add to the simple dread of another twelve hours on the road the mystery of the seating arrangements, there was plenty to occupy our playful imaginations.

It stormed during the night and we awoke to a dark and sodden landscape. Dutifully, we went to the dining room and awaited our Chinese companions. Well after the appointed breakfast hour, they had not yet arrived, so we ate hard boiled eggs that had been quartered in their shells and more of the bland bread. We heard the car pull up and the Chinese joined us and ate without ever mentioning the seating arrangements. We left first, walking in the rain, leaving the troika to a dry ride back to their rooms. After gathering all our belongings, we waited. The van then arrived with the driver at the wheel, Miss Peng in the middle row, and Miss Zhu in purdah.

The trip back was, above all, quiet. There could be few surprises, and only the certainty of that endless journey. I suspect that we secretly took heart in the inclement weather since it made stopping for photographs less likely. Even bypassing the enchanting compound at Gyantse became a bright prospect. We also took satisfaction in Miss Zhu's discomfort. At the outset, I offered her my green down jacket as a pillow with great chivalry. As the rest of us periodically rotated in the other seats, she shifted her padding with great fanfare. The driver was clearly displeased with the seating arrangements; maybe it was his bad temper that now kept him from nodding off. Frankly, we were not interested in his emotional well-being. All we wanted was to put this road trip behind us, especially as we came closer to that dreaded portion following the bridge crossing. Once over it, though, the Chinese seemed to crank up with a new burst of energy. Maybe it was the reunion between Miss Peng and Miss Zhu, the latter finally rescued from the back to share the front seat with her colleague. We just did not have the heart to leave her back there; after all, our point had been made. How they chattered! And about what? Food. It is as if Americans endlessly amused themselves by discussing Idaho potatoes or Vermont maple syrup, but only in the western context does it sound ridiculous if one remembers that a common greeting between Chinese is "Have you eaten yet?" The word "spinster" also came up, somehow becoming the focus of lively discussion, the concept of which was eventually dismissed by Misses Peng and Zhu as "grotesque."

We finally spotted the Potala but knew from experience that we still had well over an hour on the road. Then came the structure that looked like a bridge, covered with the same rocks that were to be found everywhere. What was particularly amusing about this, our third crossing, was that people were still painting the trim along the length of the whole span. There was no road bed, but shimmering grill work. Shortly past it, there was a new detour that would take us through a stream. We had to wait because a convoy was again coming from the opposite direction. For some reason, one of the trucks yet again chose to stop right on a rise immediately after crossing the rivulet, thereby forcing all those following to negotiate a difficult passage. We again watched with amusement as each truck coped with the needless hazard, but when yet another open truck brimming with splashing night soil cargo appeared to be tipping over in our direction, our amusement changed to dread.

Back in the dining room, there were a few new tables of tourists. When we straggled in, they asked if we had just made the trip from the airport. When we told of our journey from Shigatse, celebrity was ours. They, too, would be bound for Shigatse tomorrow. But how would that older woman on a crutch take aim in the privy and the fading dandy all in white cope with the horde of flies at the Shigatse watering hole? We spoke our minds and left, going down to the newly opened "club" to kill a bottle of well-traveled champagne that I had brought from Beijing. The power with which the cork popped, ricocheting wildly around the room, was worthy testimony to the whole adventure.

11

The morning of our last day was a blur, with a visit to another monastery that involved a lot of climbing. But that afternoon, we asked to go back to the free market surrounding the Jokhang Temple instead of visiting a "typical Tibetan home." Furthermore, we wanted to be dropped off by the guides and picked up at the Tibetan Medical

Hospital at six o'clock. Miss Peng simply agreed. Taking a different route into the market through rubble of newly demolished Tibetan buildings, we quickly came upon a street devoted almost entirely to yak butter. After being assaulted by the odor for a week, primarily from the monastery urns that burned the stuff, I was overwhelmed by the sight of massive chunks wrapped in yak skins on display in a film-like setting, yet I perversely forced myself to hover around it.

Further along the end of this street, we reached what seemed to be a hub with everything for purchase from saddles to gongs to rugs to leopard skins. One woman continually followed us, dredging up an unending array of jewelry from within the many folds of her costume; she also had a baby on her back. I bought two intricately embroidered saddle blankets from a Chinese merchant. A frisky old monk soon appeared, spinning the hell out of his prayer wheel and sporting a red baseball cap! As we strolled on, a young fellow demanded some personal attention. He was not selling anything; rather, he was putting money into my hand. Initially, I thought he was a beggar, illustrating what he wanted me to do. But, when he opened a cloth containing photographs of the Dalai Lama, I realized that he had hoped to buy any that I might have. He stuck with us as we left the market, holding my hand through the yak butter street and plaintively repeating the Dalai Lama's name. Finally, a Tibetan who spoke some Chinese interceded, explaining as I instructed that if I had any pictures, it would be my pleasure to give them to him. Upon hearing that, he turned and put his arms around me, and with tears in his eyes, said "Too-jay-chay" ("thank you.") After releasing me, he sent me on my way, watching me—and I him—until out of sight.

Back at our hospital rendezvous, we were relieved that the car had not yet arrived, needing some time to decompress from our wanderings in the free market. Once underway, we were reluctant to be quizzed by our minders about the price of our purchases. It was a quiet trip back to the compound for an early supper; we were to be awakened at three o'clock in the morning for the trip back to Lhasa airport.

Breakfast was at three thirty, but eating was out of the question. It was simply time to leave. We were told that a Mr. Pu was now to accompany us in the van. I was pleased that the driver no longer required the company of Miss Zhu, his muse. But upon his arrival, Mr. Pu grandly announced that a prominent local opera singer, Mr. An, would be hitching a ride with us. Furthermore, he hinted that for such a person of renown, the rear seat might not be appropriate. We mindlessly agreed and let him squeeze in front with the guide and the driver.

The trip in the darkness was a literal nightmare. With no obvious points of reference, the driver really had to rely on instinct. One wrong turn did cost us a good half hour, yet one could not blame him for it since that particular path was lined with trees much like the correct route that we had dubbed the Appian Way. But a detour of this sort was insignificant compared to the three washouts that awaited us and truly threatened our passage. At one, we were reduced to tossing stones into the rushing water to get a sense of its depth. At another, the angles down and up the banks seemed so sharp that continuing on looked impossible; and at the third, we had to navigate around a beached bus. Evidently, the earlier rains that night had been much heavier outside of Lhasa, thereby creating such treacherous conditions. By the time we reached the bridge, it was dawn, but unfortunately, the road on the other side of the river did not improve.

Once at the airport, we faced "internal customs," with the Chinese going through every zippered pocket of my bags. They were amused by the bells but took pause at the stones I had picked up at the Potala, one destined for my mother's grave. When asked why I wanted them, I replied "for fun," a very loose translation of a Chinese expression used to describe any pleasurable waste of time. They were satisfied. We were then herded into a jammed and smoke-filled waiting room, denied permission to enter the completely empty one adjacent to it. I plopped my hastily repacked bag down on the floor and leaned up against the wall, calming down from the drive and the search. A Chinese toddler walked within a foot of my possessions with a great sense of purpose and urinated. I had to sprint to get my things out of the way in time. Then, by some fluke, as we boarded the plane, Karin and I were put into first class—all by ourselves. Ignoring the stewardess' knee-jerk remark about the quality of our Chinese, I just drifted over mountains and through memories, disoriented by the prospect of returning to the very people who were ruining Tibet.

Thanksgiving

When I lived in Beijing over two decades ago as Manufacturers Hanover Trust Company's first representative, a bank name which no longer exists, I received an invitation to a state banquet to be hosted by President Reagan. Prior to the occasion, an advance party arrived, including Donald Regan, former Chair of Merrill Lynch and incumbent Secretary of the United States Treasury. The phone rang in my office. It was Ambassador Hummel's secretary asking if I would prepare a briefing for Mr. Regan. Evidently, the Secretary was keen to hear from commercial people on the ground rather than simply being handled by government functionaries. I happily accepted.

In the context of the challenges facing us as we tried to make our way in Beijing, I prepared a one-page memo dwelling on the issue of "reciprocity"—a word loaded with significance. Not only was it shamelessly bandied about during countless toasting ceremonies between Chinese and foreigners, but it also had a powerful significance in the philosophical tradition. *Bao*, the concept of reciprocity, was linked to obligations shared in relationships traditionally governing society. The word might have been cheapened by insincere usage at banquets of the day, but when used in Chinese, it conjured up shared duties which kept society securely on the rails. The latter meaning, though, would be a private pleasure when it came to my chat with the Secretary of the Treasury.

I was ushered in to see the flinty Mr. Regan who was quite eager to hear what it was like to do business in China. My litany of examples was clearly taken on board, such as the onerous regulation of foreign banks while the Bank of China competed freely against us in our own backyard, and foreign business people ghettoized in expensive hotels because the government prohibited rental of apartments while Chinese abroad were completely unrestricted by their foreign hosts. With momentum behind me, I just couldn't resist. I concluded my audience by saying that if such inequities were simply explained away as inevitable results of conflicting systems and traditions, then we must resign ourselves to continued exploitation; but if they were recognized as violations of the spirit of reciprocity, then we could link their correction to mutual self-interest that the Chinese would easily understand. My minutes of fame came to an end.

Later that day, the Secretary was giving a speech to his Chinese hosts and foreigners had been invited. Pals in the commercial section of the embassy happened to mention that they were really under the gun because Mr. Regan had insisted upon last minute and fundamental revisions of his remarks. There I then sat, hearing my own words coming right back at me, with reciprocity being translated into Chinese and conjuring up the very message that I had intended. His plagiarism delighted me!

The President's banquet was next. On the morning of that event, my phone rang again. It was a friend from the embassy, saying he would be coming over shortly with something of import to tell me. I was to meet him in the lobby of the hotel and our chat would have to be away from the windows. A bit of context: since he had something confidential to impart, the phone was no way to do it. They were all bugged. I later discovered that his request to meet away from the windows also had to do with security. The hotel's own bugging devices were most sensitive near the glass. But, the anxiety triggered by the mystery of it all was born of sudden terror unrelated to matters of state. I feared that he was coming to shoot me. Though gay, I was nonetheless smitten with his wife, a glamorous and sweet attorney who looked like Gena Rowlands. There I stood, in the middle of the entrance hall, awaiting my fate as he arrived.

"You have been chosen to sit at the President's table tonight, but you can tell no one." He then handed me an envelope with a special sticker for the car and was on his way.

I took the matter of confidentiality most seriously. It was only after I was seated in the car did I hand Mr. Qi the sticker and confide the secret of our destination—The Great Wall Hotel. The security there was tight, but we were waved in, passing many sentries along the way. Mr. Qi was delighted by our treatment. At the entrance, I said good-bye and was immediately surrounded by several chaps who ushered me in through a special door to a metal detector. With great courtesy, they confirmed my honor of sitting with the President and listed some of the other guests at the table: Ambassador Hummel, Madam Chen Muhua, Minister for Foreign Economic Relations and Trade, and Premier Zhao Ziyang himself (later purged after the Tiananmen Massacre for empathizing with the demonstrators). I was then personally escorted to table five in the huge banquet hall and asked to remain standing.

I suddenly became aware of an elderly gentleman milling about. He seemed to lock on to me, his milling gradually becoming more strategic. "You're in my seat," he barked. I actually thought he was talking to someone else. He repeated himself, and as he did so, I recognized him: Dr. Armand Hammer, the oil baron from California, notorious for his obsession with stardom—not mine, but clearly with Ronald Reagan's. I courteously declined to swap seats, and he continued bullying. Finally, someone appeared and saw him away; and no sooner was he gone then the President arrived.

Even before sitting down, Mr. Reagan confessed with a wink that he had forgotten his hearing aid and wouldn't be able to understand a word said all night. We had a good chuckle, and I was immediately disarmed by his lack of vanity. A Chinese Nobel laureate was to my left and Madam Chen to my right. The Ambassador and the Premier, in their places opposite me, were shadowed by interpreters. The table was now complete. The matter immediately raised by our Chinese guests was the number of the table: how could the head table not be number one? Add to traditional notions of status the current use of numbers to signify both identity and station—I was Jianguo Hotel Room Number 114 (*jianguo fandian yao yao si*) rather than Peter Lighte—and their disorientation at so American a gesture of democracy could be appreciated.

In these early days of Chinese familiarity with western customs, the array of silverware and wine glasses must have been daunting to our guests. I took great pains to exaggerate choice and usage of implements as the meal began. Despite my efforts, Madam Chen was soon seen balancing her entire salmon mousse on a knife, inhaling it mighty neatly. The finest Californian wines were being served, but that could never be known since each bottle was completely wrapped like a newborn in a crisp napkin, obviously in keeping with some Swiss sommelier's notion of class. Anyway, the glasses were knocked back randomly, with no vintage chit-chat at this gathering. Along with the wines, American fare was served; and when the tasteful and meager plates of turkey arrived, Premier Zhao asked me if it was as precious to Americans as shark's fin was to the Chinese. I dutifully fielded and passed on the query to which the President offered back the significance of the bird, couched in the context of Thanksgiving. As I knew when the exchange began, precious in one language did not mean precious in another. The Premier wanted to know price per pound and the President was talking about a pilgrim's progress. I must confess that I shamelessly inflated the price when responding— and that is why I can never be an interpreter.

The evening stayed lively, with not a hint of deafness afflicting the host. As the plates were being cleared away, the Nobel laureate nudged me and commented, "No noodles?" Next to my plate was a souvenir pack of cigarettes bearing the presidential seal, which I put in my pocket. After our guests departed, I brushed past Dr. Hammer and wished him a good evening, and was again taken in hand by security and brought to my car. Mr. Qi was simply thrilled by our special treatment—including right of way on every street—which was clearly causing tremendous inconvenience throughout the city. This capitalist was feeling for the people harassed by police and barricades while the worker was gloating over their very trials. As Mr. Qi stopped in front of the Jianguo to drop me off, I handed him that pack of cigarettes. Considering that the ordinary variety was still very much a currency of its own back in a China just recovering from the

Cultural Revolution, that souvenir of our special evening was off the charts.

A few days later, that phone rang again. It was the bank chairman's secretary. "Mr. McGillicuddy would like to speak with you," Virginia said.

"I hear you're coming to the States on home leave soon," he warmly bellowed.

He wanted a favor. "Can I ask you to pass through California on your way to New York?"

No problem, I assured him, not yet over the shock of his call.

"We need to go and see a client together. He's obsessed with China and wants to pick our brains. You know Armand Hammer, don't you?"

Half The Sky

All profits from *Pieces of China* will be donated to Half The Sky, a foundation which seeks to bring a caring adult into the life of each orphan in China (see www.halfthesky.org).

4221762

Made in the USA
Lexington, KY
04 January 2010